Visual Experiences

A CONCISE GUIDE TO DIGITAL INTERFACE DESIGN

T0134115

Visual Experiences

A CONCISE GUIDE TO DIGITAL INTERFACE DESIGN

Carla Viviana Coleman

CRC Press
Taylor & Francis Group
Boca Raton London New York

CRC Press is an imprint of the
Taylor & Francis Group, an **informa** business

A CHAPMAN & HALL BOOK

CRC Press
Taylor & Francis Group
6000 Broken Sound Parkway NW, Suite 300
Boca Raton, FL 33487-2742

International Standard Book Number-13: 978-1-4987-7053-8 (Paperback)
978-1-1387-1914-9 (Hardback)

Library of Congress Cataloging-in-Publication Data

Names: Coleman, Carla Viviana, author.
Title: Visual experiences : a concise guide to digital interface design /
Carla Viviana Coleman.
Description: Boca Raton : Taylor & Francis, CRC Press, 2017. | Includes
bibliographical references.
Identifiers: LCCN 2017001611| ISBN 9781498770538 (pbk. : alk. paper) | ISBN
9781138719149 (hardback : alk. paper)
Subjects: LCSH: User interfaces (Computer systems)--Design.
Classification: LCC QA76.9.U83 C59 2017 | DDC 005.4/37--dc23
LC record available at https://lccn.loc.gov/2017001611

Visit the Taylor & Francis Web site at
http://www.taylorandfrancis.com

and the CRC Press Web site at
http://www.crcpress.com

Printed and bound in the United States of America by Sheridan

Contents

Section I Thinking

Section II   Design

Section III   Interaction

Author

Carla Viviana Coleman is an educator, researcher, writer, and designer. Her work has been featured in the books *Indie Publishing* (2008) and *Graphic Design: The New Basics* (2008), both published by Princeton Architectural Press. She owns, edits, and maintains the website www.webtypography.org, which is part of her book titled *Web Typography: A Handbook for Graphic Designers* (2012), published by Createspace. Her work has been exhibited in The Siggraph Exhibition Conference, Ssamzie Space, Gallery 175 in Seoul, South Korea, and others. She served on the Board of Directors of AIGA Baltimore. She also co-authored, along with Yeohyun Ahn, *Type and Code: Processing for Designers* (2009), published by MICA—Maryland Institute College of Art.

SECTION I
Thinking

Evolution of Digital Design
Interfaces

1876–1945: Before Interfaces	1990–2000
1945–1970	2013–2020
1980–1990	References

1876–1945: Before Interfaces

Various inventions and essays inspired the creation of the graphical user interface (GUI). On March 10, 1876, Alexander Graham Bell (Figure 1.1) made the first phone call (Raum 2008), changing communications history forever. From that moment, we had a new way of communicating without participating in a face-to-face conversation. Around the same time, in 1888, the first patent was issued for an electrical stylus device for capturing handwriting (Figure 1.2), and a few decades later, in 1915, a handwriting recognition user interface with a stylus was created, on which the analog tablet was based (Figure 1.3).

Television was also invented during the same era, and the first international broadcast of a recorded signal occurred in 1928, sent between London and New York. Black-and-white pictures progressed to color in 1953 (Figure 1.4), and the next step was the creation of the wireless remote control for televisions, which was developed by Eugene Polley in 1955, giving viewers more control over their televisions without requiring close physical proximity to the set (Marschall 1986).

The way in which we interact with information has thus changed drastically since the telephone and television were invented, yet these artifacts and others

3

Figure 1.1

Alexander Graham Bell. (Courtesy of Gilbert H. Grosvenor Collection, 1892, https://en.wikipedia.org/wiki/Alexander_Graham_Bell#/media/File:Alexander_Graham_Telephone_in_Newyork.jpg)

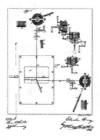

Figure 1.2

Electrical stylus device. (Courtesy of Elisha Gray, 2015.)

Figure 1.3

Hand recognition user interface. (Courtesy of Ed Bernar, 2015, https://www.sutori.com/story/history-of-pen-computing.)

provided some of the inspiration for later interface designs, given the very limited means of communicating prior to the 1800s.

Modern computers were invented in 1936 by Konrad Zuse, who created the first binary computer for a mechanical calculator named *Z1* (Figure 1.5). This started a revolution, and in 1941 version Z3 was launched, which had most of the capabilities of a modern computer, albeit with the limitation of a 64-word memory, which affected its ability to save information.

Figure 1.4

Color television. (Courtesy of Envisioning the American Dream. *The Case of the Vanished Vision.* Available at: https://envisioningtheamericandream. com/2014/11/13/the-case-of-the-vanished-vision/.)

Figure 1.5

Z1 invented by Konrad Kuze. (Courtesy of Construction of the Z1 in the apartment of Zuse's parent. Available at: http://history-computer.com/ModernComputer/ Relays/Zuse.html)

As modern computing evolved, this new device trained its users to think, work, analyze, save, calculate, and investigate information in a new way (Randell 1973), and as a consequence computers would never be the same again. Users started to depend on computers, which in earlier times had occupied large rooms (e.g., the UNIVAC system; Figure 1.6). But the computer and television screen came together to create a user interface that helped individuals access, save, and retrieve data, be entertained and entertain others, and much more. The television, which displays visuals and sound, was married to the computer, which provided the brain for the combined device.

This technological revolution occurred rapidly from the mid-1800s to the mid-1900s. Every artifact helped inspire, create, and build the next invention, until eventually GUIs were created. If a problem remained unresolved, the next generation would solve it.

Figure 1.6

UNIVAC system. (Courtesy of George Michael, 2015, http://www.computer-history. info/Page4.dir/pages/Univac.dir/images/Picture.7.jpg.)

1945–1970

1945: Vannevar Bush and His Memex Project

In July 1945, Vannevar Bush (1945) wrote an article entitled "As We May Think," which inspired the eventual creation of interfaces. In this article, he mentioned his memex project and described how users would be able to retrieve, access, and save information in the future. The name *memex* came from the union of two words, *memory* and *index*. The project was a physical desktop that contained various types of helpful tools to access information, including three information/image displays, each of which could be used to search, retrieve, copy, paste, and save information by using an analog interface (Figure 1.7) that completed all tasks in a matter of seconds. Further, information could be saved in small artifacts and placed in a drawer of the desktop. This groundbreaking article opened the eyes of many inventors and researchers of the period, helping them to deal with information in the future.

MEMEX in the form of a desk would instantly bring files and material on any subject to the operator's fingertips. Slanting translucent viewing screens magnify supermicro-film filed by code numbers. At left is a mechanism which automatically photographs longhand notes, pictures and letters, then files them in the desk for future reference.

AS WE MAY THINK CONTINUED

Figure 1.7

The memex project. (Courtesy of Tom Davidson, 2015, http://www.tjdav.me.uk/ memex-research-project/2015/10/07/.)

1968: Douglas Engelbart

A few decades after the memex project, which was realized in the actual computing technology of that time, Douglas Engelbart gave a seminal presentation in 1968 regarding what could be achieved by using augmented science research computing. He presented a variety of new inventions, including the mouse, hypertext, object addressing, dynamic file linking, shared screen collaboration, and communication over a network with an audio and video interface, and the extent of his innovation astonished the audience. This presentation was an essential factor behind what was to come in the commercial world a few decades later (Figure 1.8). Indeed, it was the first computer screen tutorial with the first prototype interface to use a mouse, including functions that we now perform on a daily basis.

1973: Xerox Alto

In 1973, the Xerox Alto (Figure 1.9) was built, but at the time it was only known to the research world. This computer was unique, and it is recognized today as one of the first personal computers. During the creation of the Xerox Alto at Xerox PARC, its inventors realized that they needed a file manager and user interface to create applications for the computer (Wadlow 1981). Prior to this personal computer interface, tasks were given directly through coding and text-line commands to the popular operating system on the market at that time (i.e., disk operating system, or DOS). The inventors of the Xerox Alto needed to create a new programming language, because the DOS was very limited, and as such they created a new visual code called *Smalltalk*. Owing to the memory capacity of the first GUI (Figure 1.10), the interface design was limited to a black-and-white display, a few sizes of text, low image resolution, a few metaphorical graphical icons (e.g., desktop, time, calendar), mostly text-based navigation, overlapping windows, and an early version of layering of tasks on the desktop.

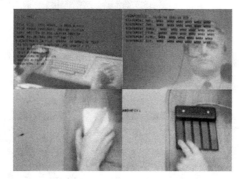

Figure 1.8

Douglas Engelbart's presentation. (Courtesy of Doug Engelbart Institute, 1968, https://www.youtube.com/watch?v=JfIgzSoTMOs.)

Figure 1.9

Xerox Alto. (Courtesy of Computer History Museum, 2015, http://www.computer history.org/revolution/input-output/14/347.)

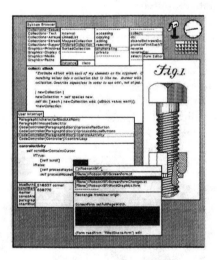

Figure 1.10

Graphical user interface of Xerox Alto. (Courtesy of Arstechnica, 2016, https://cdn. arstechnica.net/images/gui/7-AltoST.jpg.)

1974: Smalltalk

Smalltalk was the first visual programming language in history, a modern and visual Integrated Development Environment (IDE) composed of a GUI (Figure 1.11), debugger (to fix programming language problems), compiler (to gather all code), and code editor (to edit the code). Nowadays we have hundreds of IDE programming

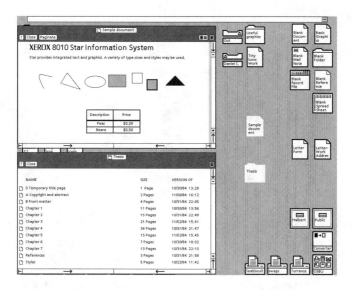

Figure 1.11

GUI using Smalltalk. (Courtesy of Toastytech, 2015, http://toastytech.com/guis/
starbitmap2.gif.)

languages, but before Smalltalk most computers used DOS, and there was no GUI
on the computer. This innovative object-oriented programming language had similar features to Java. DOS was operated by code or text commands to obtain results
through hierarchical directories. On the other hand, Smalltalk provided a GUI that
allowed users to create icons, scrollbars, radio buttons, dialog boxes, windows, a
visual desktop, and other levels of layers to demonstrate a visual hierarchy for the first
time. This groundbreaking invention was thus the beginning of the era of the GUI.

1980–1990

Xerox PARC heralded a new era with the Xerox Star in 1981 (Johnson et al.
1999). Several sketches show how the interface was to be organized prior to the
final design decisions, including an early sketch of the GUI "mail" application
(Figure 1.12), which shows a complex illustration that would have taken too much
of the screen resolution (Wadlow 1981). However, designers lacked the knowledge and their icons were limited. A team of user interface designers comprising
Bill Bowman, Norm Cox, Wallace Judd, and Dave Smith designed most of the
interface, which was then tested by users and adjusted according to their feedback. This interface was the first to be tested and analyzed by the general public.

This computer model made a groundbreaking entrance as a business and
personal computer (i.e., a document editor), and its GUI offered icons for objects,
applications, and files. Moreover, the background of the main screen became the
user's virtual desktop, where documents were displayed, and move, copy, and
delete functions were provided as well. The user interface included windows,

Figure 1.12

Early sketch for a mail icon. (Courtesy of Norm Cox, 2015, http://www.digibarn.com/collections/software/xerox-star/xerox-world-according-to-norm_files/star-incoming-mail.jpg.)

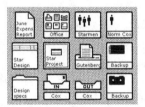

Figure 1.13

Cox, The (Xerox Star Icon) World According to Norm Cox. Digibarn Computer Museum, California. (Courtesy of Digibarn Computer Museum, Boulder Creek, CA, http://www.digibarn.com/collections/software/xerox-star/xerox-world-according-to-norm.html.)

scroll bars, a black-and-white screen, a virtual keyboard, and an option to send to a printer. The resolution of the computer interface was 72 × 72 pixels per inch because the printer was 72 × 72 points per inch. This allowed easy calculation between the screen and the printer, especially useful for typesetting and typography. The provided resolution was high enough to change the text from 8 to 72 points, and the maximum number of points on the screen was 300, equal to a printed piece of paper. In addition, the GUI was "what you see is what you get" (WYSIWYG) (Figure 1.14), meaning that printed documents mirrored what was seen on the screen. Typefaces had extremely limited availability (one to eight options) and quantity. The Xerox Star also had a bitmapped display that presented characters, images, and the GUI proportionally.

The Xerox Star had a word processor, spreadsheets, and other applications that revolutionized desktop work, and the GUI of the applications and

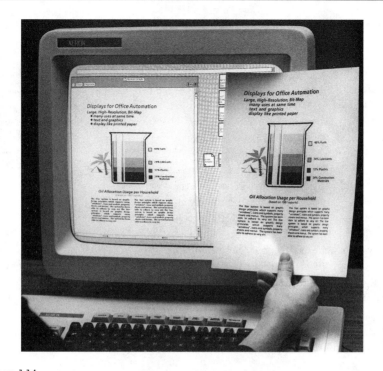

Figure 1.14

WYSIWYG. (Courtesy of Pinterest, 2015, https://s-media-cache-ak0.pinimg.com/736x/63/8d/8d/638d8db30c1e40aa83602807465883cc.jpg.)

operating system was cohesive in their layout, typeface, and branding across the entire computer. Although the cost of this computer was extremely high, Xerox was able to sell thousands of units.

Overall, during the creation of the GUI for the Xerox Star and its applications, graphic designers set rules and guidelines that had not existed before (i.e., the visual order on the screen and user focus groups needed to test to see whether the design had been seen in other graphic design projects). Most graphic designers were working in the print field, making books, posters, and other print projects with limited technology (and usually by hand). Their work typically involved manually transferring lettering or Zipatone lettering.

Graphic designers creating GUIs used their design intuition, guided by the limitations of computer technology, and made revisions as a result of feedback from user testing. It is important to recognize that these designers were breaking new ground and thus creating a new academic discipline: user interface design.

1983: Apple Lisa

After much lab research, a revolutionary computer named the Apple Lisa was released on January 19, 1983, introducing the market to a computer with an esthetically pleasing GUI and mouse. Moreover, the computer screen provided drop-down menus and pictographic icons for the first time (Figure 1.15). Susan Kare designed the GUI of the Apple Lisa, which was then developed by the Apple team. Kare designed a wide range of graphics at Apple (Figure 1.16), and her attention to detail, which began from the sketching process, was extremely important because all the graphic icons were restricted to 32 × 32 pixels in a black-and-white range, which is very limited compared with today's resolutions (Kare 2011). The computer had a typeface designed especially for this system called *Chicago* (Figure 1.17a), and its resolution was 720 × 364 pixels horizontally and vertically, which was revolutionary compared with other screens that were at most 80% of the resolution of this Macintosh computer.

The GUI of the Lisa was cohesive from the desktop to the applications. Its simple metaphoric icons, which were beautifully created, were limited to pixilated graphics and thus the creativity behind all the icons was extremely ambitious for its time. In addition, the use of gray in between black and white provided a good contrast and was well chosen, because these colors increased the visibility of the icons and text on the screen when layering windows on the desktop platform. Hierarchy throughout the system was executed effectively by providing users with a lot of freedom (relative to other interfaces of the time) to move and drag windows and alter their size (maximizing and minimizing); however, this was a very challenging task to execute. The Apple Lisa set a new competitive standard at that time, and its users praised the quality of its hardware and software, including its GUI.

Figure 1.15

Apple Lisa computer. (Courtesy of oldcomputers.net, 2015, http://oldcomputers. net/pics/lisa2.jpg.)

Figure 1.16

Icons designed by Susan Kare. (Courtesy of Susan Kare Graphic Design, http:// kare.com/apple-icons/.)

1. Evolution of Digital Design

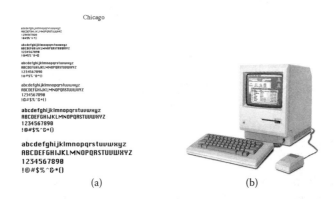

Chicago

(a)   (b)

Figure 1.17

(a) Chicago typeface. (b) Mac II. (Courtesy of Master's Tech, 2015, http://www.masterstech-home.com/Images/Font_Sample_Gifs/C/Chicago.GIF.)

1987: Mac II

This system provided color for the first time upon its introduction in 1987 (Figure 1.17b), with up to 16.7 million different shades from which to choose and a large memory capacity never before offered on a personal computer. Having a color screen elevated graphics to a whole new level, ending the limitations of black-and-white systems, abstract bitmap icons, and typography and ushering in a new age. During this period, desktop publishing, design, and art software were also introduced, resulting in significantly more choice for graphic designers and artists in terms of tools when they began to do their work on computers.

The low cost of Macs democratized computers, as it provided the opportunity for most people to buy a computer system with a groundbreaking user interface and a color monitor with 16-color display. Learning the interface was easy, as was access. Through tutorials on how to work in the GUI, it usually took around 60–120 minutes to learn the applications and computer system. Because this computer was cheap, however, it had less memory (128k), and as such programmers had to reprogram the entire GUI system from the Apple II to allow it to run successfully on a computer with less memory. The resolutions of this computer's display were 512×384 and 640×480.

Demand for computers and software exploded in the early 1980s, with several companies emerging such as Vision Tandy, DeskMate, Microsoft, Amiga 1000, GEM 1.0, GEOS, Arthur, and NeXTSTEP. Ultimately, however, only Microsoft Windows succeeded in the market because the others lacked an effective product design, although Apple bought NeXTSTEP in 1997, thus enabling it to survive.

Adobe Software

Besides Microsoft software, Adobe wrote some of the first pieces of software to successfully reach the masses and help the world share ideas and information by using creative software tools on personal computers. In 1984, Postscript was released (Figure 1.18). Two years later, Adobe went public and Postscript

Figure 1.18

Postscript printer by Wikipedia. (Courtesy of Wikipedia, 2016, https://en.wikipedia.org/wiki/LaserWriter)

became the general language for images and text that needed to be printed. It was a revolutionary time because Postscript changed the way designers and artists created work and removed limits to rotating text, layers, color, and scale during the design process, ultimately making it easy to send work to the printer.

In 1987 and 1988, Adobe Illustrator and Photoshop were introduced, changing the mindset of creative users. These pieces of software (Figures 1.19 and 1.20) were the first of their kind, providing a set of iconic tools, a virtual document, and a large set of options to adjust vectors and pixels. The new virtual environment extended beyond a user's desktop, provided applications, and opened up a whole new virtual set of tools. Applications started to become extremely popular, and creative people were needed to create GUIs as more and more applications were being created and sold over time.

Figure 1.19

First Adobe Illustrator GUI.

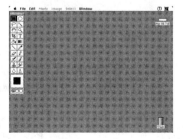

Figure 1.20

First Adobe Photoshop GUI.

The market for GUIs expanded in the 1980s to include a wide range of fields such as medicine, education, and entertainment, to name but a few. For example, Mathematica, released in 1988, was an application geared toward mathematical computation and created by mathematicians and scientists (Jones 2014). The GUIs of increasingly complex software applications were created by teams in order to evaluate all their tools and functions.

Most user interfaces (Figure 1.21) were not as successful as that of Apple, largely due to the fact that screen colors were limited and their selections were not user-friendly. Furthermore, the brightness of the screen colors posed a threat to users' vision if they stared at them for long periods of time. In addition, the grid and hierarchy of the systems were disorganized, and most tried to mimic the GUI of Apple computers.

After the collapse of most of the companies mentioned above, Microsoft created Windows 3.0 and 3.1 between 1990 and 1992, which were very successful partly due to the collaboration of Kare, who had designed the user interface for the Apple Lisa. The GUI developed for Windows by Kare was beautifully designed and executed (Figure 1.22). In addition, Kare is well known for creating the interface of the

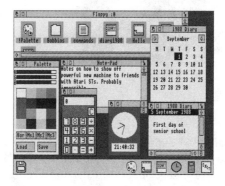

Figure 1.21

Acorn GUI computers.

Figure 1.22

Icons for Windows 3.0 designed by Susan Kare.

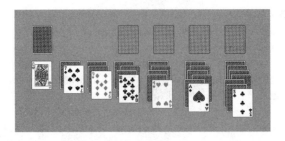

Figure 1.23

Solitaire game interface designed by Susan Kare. (Courtesy of Susan Kare, 2016, http://kare.com/microsoft/)

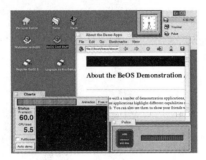

Figure 1.24

BeOS.

game Solitaire (Figure 1.23). Simultaneously, Apple created OS 2.0, which allowed users to install Windows on a Mac, although this necessitated some minor changes to the interface, such as a change of pointer color and shape when hovering.

In 1991, more competition arrived in this industry with BeOS, although this product only lasted for a short period (Figure 1.24). Eight years later, the market witnessed the release of GNOME, an open-source operating system that remains active, updating new releases for its users.

1990–2000

The age of responsiveness exploded in the early 1990s, as various companies created devices with differing screen sizes. For example, in 1991, the PowerBook 100 was introduced in 1991 (Figure 1.25). It did not sell well because it weighed 16 lbs and was thus too heavy to carry around. Apple then created the iMac in 1998, while the Mac OS 6 (Figure 1.26) provided new applications such as MacPaint, WordPerfect Works, Microsoft Basic, and MacWrite. According to consumer reports, this Mac was one of the fastest and smallest of its kind compared with a PC of the same qualities, and its operating system was exceptional. Two years later, Apple went on to create Aqua.

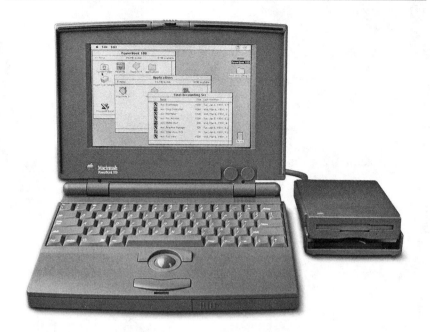

Figure 1.25

PowerBook 100. (Courtesy of Wikipedia, 2016, https://en.wikipedia.org/wiki/
PowerBook_100)

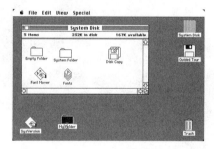

Figure 1.26

Mac OS 6.

2000

Finally, the groundbreaking application iTunes appeared on the market in 2000
(Figure 1.27) and, along with the release of the first iPod in 2001 (Figure 1.28),
it made history in terms of how users interact with devices. The small-screened
iPod was a device that allowed its user to listen to his or her favorite music. It
rapidly became very popular for use while walking, dancing, running, and working out. The interface was simple, comprising a few icons and using step-by-step
text-based and scroll-wheel navigation.

Figure 1.27

iTunes version 1.

Figure 1.28

iPod. (Courtesy of Apple, 2016, https://www.apple.com/ipod/)

The year 2001 also witnessed the launch of the tablet PC. Then, in 2007, sales of small handheld devices with responsive applications and interfaces exploded with the arrival of the iPhone and its many applications and novel technologies. By 2010, the iPad (Figure 1.29) and Galaxy Tab (Figure 1.30) had been introduced as well, and since then various other brands have created their own versions of smartphones and tablets (Keramidas 2015).

Figure 1.29

iPad. (Courtesy of Apple, 2016, https://www.apple.com/ipad/)

Figure 1.30

Nexus 1 phone made by Android, Google, and HTC. (Courtesy of Android, 2016, https://www.google.com/nexus/)

GUIs have not only been created as operating systems for computers and devices but have also become popular as the applications of third parties have been installed on computers and devices. The largest growth and creation of applications started when iPhone and Android phones went on sale. The App Store (Figure 1.31) and Google Play (Figure 1.32) currently provide millions of apps for desktops, handheld devices, wearable devices, and much more, from operating systems to calendar applications. All of these require a user interface, and their GUIs must be transparent in order to provide their users with clear and concise interaction.

As new software and devices are increasingly created, the need for exceptional interface design has become crucial in the market. The need for transparency within the visual identity of the application or any type of software will determine part of the success of the software, whether it is an operating system in a device or a game application. Therefore, the process of understanding how to give a user a successful experience through an interface has become very competitive.

Another major player has been the Internet, which allows information to be shared globally through web pages that have become more responsive and

Figure 1.31

iTunes Store.

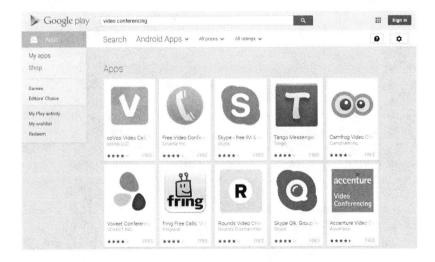

Figure 1.32

Google Play Store.

complex over time (i.e., WordPress [Figure 1.33], Blackboard, Facebook, and Zoho [Figure 1.34]). The interfaces of websites and devices have overlapped, because both share the new cloud technologies that are changing the way we save and share our files.

Interface design for websites or web apps is also extremely important in the evolution of visual experiences. As technology matures, we will see better interface design—for example, more flexibility with the use of typography on the web and effective, responsive design. Overall, users today are living in an age that is setting the standards for various types of technologies that require interfaces.

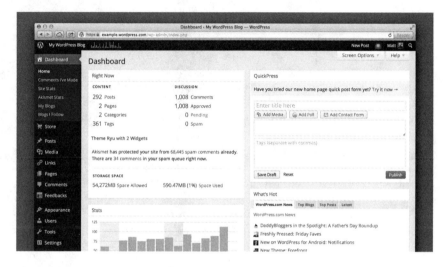

Figure 1.33

WordPress application.

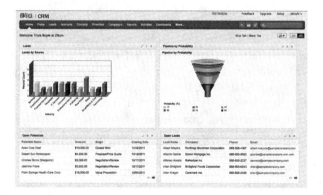

Figure 1.34

Zoho application.

Figure 1.35

Adobe Creative Cloud.

The democratization of cloud computing opened up new doors to application giants such as Adobe (Figure 1.35), which offered users the opportunity to use its cloud services on a monthly basis rather than buying a software package that would last only a year. Although it is possible to cancel the new Adobe service anytime, users never actually own the application because it is updated constantly. Many other application services have similarly opted to use cloud computing because of its security and freedom to update software on an ongoing basis.

Cloud computing is another type of interface that needs to be further developed, and with the help of users the interfaces will become extremely transparent and easy to manage over time.

2013–2020

Rigorous research has been conducted on the topic of wearable computing over the years, especially the groundbreaking presentation of Douglas Engelbart's one-handed chording keyboard in oN-Line System (NLS) (online system) (Gust 2006). Since then this technology has evolved, and a major step in wearable technology available to the public market has been a GUI within the Apple Watch (Figure 1.36), released in September 2014. Other wearable interfaces have not been as successful, yet the Apple Watch has changed users' lives by supplementing handheld devices. In 2013, the wearable device market took another step forward with the release of Google Glass (Figure 1.37) and again in 2016 with Microsoft's HoloLens (Figure 1.38). Both of these glasses have thus far only been released to developers and are not available to wider consumers as of yet (Microsoft n.d.).

The interface design of new devices such as the Apple Watch and Google Glass uses the smallest screen sizes ever created for user interactive experience. The new design fundamentals for these types of wearable interfaces differ from

Figure 1.36

Apple Watch. (Courtesy of Apple, 2016, https://www.apple.com/watch/)

Figure 1.37

Google Glass. (Courtesy of Microsoft, 2016, https://www.google.com/glass/start/)

Figure 1.38

HoloLens by Microsoft. (Courtesy of Microsoft, 2016, https://www.microsoft.com/en-us/hololens/developers)

what has been done so far in terms of icons, menus, gestures, and typography, because past devices were used with less movement. But having devices that become body accessories demands more visual creativity and organization when creating visual functions that will enable the user to have a good experience of the design of an application, website, or software.

HoloLens is also a new wearable device that is not limited to a single screen size and even creates a 3D environment. This new technology is breaking the barriers to limited screen sizes in devices and instead is using the physical world. Interface design will face new challenges when this technology becomes readily available when using applications, searching the web, or accessing any other kind of information. Overall, technological breakthroughs continually happen and interface design has to keep up with the progression, as the screen limits are off and the future brings boundless user experiences.

The expansion and research of GUIs have become unlimited due to the urgent need for interfaces in this information age. GUIs have drastically changed the way we interact, create, analyze, work, and communicate with the world around us. They are in our phones, tablets, computers, and even our glasses. They have become a necessity in our fast-paced lives because we are now able to use gestures, virtual reality, sound, speech, and much more to easily command a task and get it done.

As technology evolves, we constantly see solutions for displaying visual information through user interfaces. Generation Z has been introduced to user interfaces from a very early age through games, apps, books, and songs. They do not see an interface as a tool but rather as an extension of themselves. The next step for GUI designers is to understand the needs of users and find better ways to help them handle information. Technology is evolving to become part of us, since in the future we are likely to see chips implanted into our brains in order to enable our thoughts to control our environment (Jin et al. 2012) (Figure 1.39). As such, we are beginning to embed technology into our bodies. This advancement will change the way we think and share information, taking it to a new level.

Figure 1.39

BCI brain–computer interface. (Courtesy of Multimedia Signal Processing Group MMSPG, 2016, http://mmspg.epfl.ch/page-58318-en.html)

References

Anchorage Museum of History Art, and Patric Prince Archive. 1993. *Through My Window*. Anchorage, AL: Anchorage Museum of History and Art.

Campbell-Kelly, Martin, and Daniel D. Garcia-Swartz. 2015. *From Mainframes to Smartphones: A History of the International Computer Industry*. Harvard University press, 1st ed. Cambridge, Mass. London.

Cardoso Llach, Daniel. 2015. *Builders of the Vision: Software and the Imagination of Design*. Routledge, New York.

Chen, Brian X. 2009. Gallery: Tablet Computing from 1888 to 2010. *WIRED*. Last modified September 28, 2009. http://www.wired.com/2009/09/tablet-taxonomy/.

Crockett, Zachary. 2014. The Woman Behind Apple's First Icons. *Priceonomics*. Last modified April 3, 2014. http://priceonomics.com/the-woman-behind-apples-first-icons/.

Dill, Erin. 2010. The History of Adobe Illustrator. *Vecteezy*. Last modified May 24, 2010. http://www.vecteezy.com/blog/2010/5/24/the-history-of-adobe-illustrator.

Fekete, Gyorgy. 2009. Operating System Interface Design between 1981–2009. *Web Designer Depot*. Last modified March 11, 2009. http://www.webdesignerdepot.com/2009/03/operating-system-interface-design-between-1981-2009/.

Gust, Kathe. 2006. NLS Augment Index. *Software Preservation Group*. Last modified November 6, 2006. http://www.softwarepreservation.org/projects/nlsproject/.

Jin, Jing, Brendan Z. Allison, Xingyu Wang, and Christa Neuper. 2012. A combined brain–computer interface based on P300 potentials and motion-onset visual evoked potentials. *Journal of Neuroscience Methods* 205, no. 2: 265–276. doi:10.1016/j.jneumeth.2012.01.004.

Johnson, Jeff, Teresa L. Roberts, William Verplank, David C. Smith, Charles Irby, Marian Beard, and Kevin Mackey. 1999. Digibarn Documents: The Xerox Star: A Retrospective. *The DigiBarn Computer Museum*. Last modified 1999. http://www.digibarn.com/friends/curbow/star/retrospect/.

Jones, Capers. 2014. *The Technical and Social History of Software Engineering*. 2014, Upper Saddle River, NJ: Addison-Wesley.

Kare, Susan D. 2011. *Icons: Selected Work from 1983–2011*. [Place of publication not identified]: Kareprints.com.

Keramidas, Kimon. 2015. *The Interface Experience: A User's Guide*. New York: Bard Graduate Center: Decorative Arts, Design History, Material Culture.

Limer, Eric. 2013. Check Out the Whole History of Display Resolutions in One Big Stack. *Gizmodo*. Last modified February 24, 2013. http://gizmodo.com/5986520/check-out-the-whole-history-of-display-resolutions-in-one-big-stack.

Marschall, Richard. 1986. *The History of Television*. New York: Gallery Books.

Microsoft. n.d. Microsoft HoloLens | Official Site. *Microsoft HoloLens*. Accessed January 4, 2016. https://www.microsoft.com/microsoft-hololens/en-us.

Pandit, Milind, S. 1993. *How Computers Really Work*. Berkeley, CA: Osborne McGraw-Hill.

Pierce, David. 2015. Review: Apple iPad Pro. *WIRED*. Last modified November 11, 2015. http://www.wired.com/2015/11/apple-ipad-pro-review/.

Randell, Brian. 1973. *The Origins of Digital Computers: Selected Papers*. Berlin, Germany: Springer-Verlag.

Raum, Elizabeth. 2008. *The History of the Telephone*. Chicago, IL: Heinemann Library.

Reimer, Jeremy. 2005. *A History of the GUI. Ars Technica*. Last modified May 5, 2005. http://arstechnica.com/features/2005/05/gui/3/.

Stengel, Steven. 2016. Apple Lisa. *Old Computers*. Last modified December 10, 2013. http://www.oldcomputers.net/lisa.html.

Vannevar Bush. 1945. https://www.theatlantic.com/magazine/archive/1945/07/as-we-may-think/303881/ Accessed January, 2016.

Wadlow, Thomas A. 1981. DigiBarn Software: Xerox Alto Operating System and Alto Applications. *The DigiBarn Computer Museum*. Last modified September 1981. http://www.digibarn.com/collections/software/alto/.

2

User Research

Card Sorting

Contextual Interviews

First-Click Testing

Focus Group

Heuristics for User

Interface Design

Parallel Design

Personas

Prototyping

Online Surveys

System Usability Scale

Task Analysis

Use Cases

Usability Testing

References

User Research is one of the first steps when a visual designer starts to plan the entire process, and it has two main methods: qualitative and quantitative. For further information on these topics, please see Chapter 13.

The first question is always, who is our audience? Who is going to use this interface? Once we have narrowed down all the options, we select the main audience. In addition, a wide set of questions need answers before we start prototyping, some of which are as follows:

1. What is the purpose of the interface?
2. What is the project's budget and timeline?
3. Is this a long- or short-term project?
4. Why is this needed?
5. Are there any competing products in the same market?
6. Why should the user choose this product over others, if any?
7. Does the interface provide any main tools that highlight the visual experience?

By answering the questions above, the designer or design team will get a good head start on the project, whether it be a website, app, game, or large software system. In the early stages, it is also important to define a timeline and build the technical environment.

In large projects, it is advisable to hire experts on usability and statistics, since successful user evaluation requires professional help. While interface designers must have knowledge of usability and user research, they do not necessarily need to be experts in those fields. Sometimes, companies expect the developer to know everything, including visual design and usability, which is not realistic. Only a few people master various fields, so it is important to work in a team with a user researcher, interface designer, user experience researcher, developer, marketing specialist, and so on. Every member of the team is as important as the others, since each possesses a specialty that strengthens the project from beginning to end.

Overall, this chapter covers types of usability, providing interface designers with a concise analysis of each type. Interface designers must understand usability studies so that they can make successful product-design decisions. One user testing session with one user is insufficient to define an entire project; several are necessary throughout, and the interface designer must consider all the users' needs. The product is not for the interface designer but for the user, so all comments and user research decisions must be seriously considered during design. User research is applied throughout the entire design process.

A wide range of methods may be applied at various stages in the design and development process, as outlined in Figures 2.1 and 2.2.

Ideal Process Example

USER RESEARCH > INTERFACE DESIGN > DEVELOPER > FINAL PRODUCT

Figure 2.1

Thinking process from beginning to end with no interruption.

Real Process Example

USER RESEARCH > INTERFACE DESIGN > USER RESEARCH >
INTERFACE DESIGN > USER RESEARCH > INTERFACE DESIGN >
USER RESEARCH > INTERFACE DESIGN > USER RESEARCH >
INTERFACE DESIGN > USER RESEARCH > INTERFACE DESIGN >
DEVELOPER > USER RESEARCH > DEVELOPER > USER RESEARCH
> USER RESEARCH > DEVELOPER > USER RESEARCH >
INTERFACE DESIGN > USER RESEARCH > DEVELOPER >
USER RESEARCH > FINAL PRODUCT

Figure 2.2

Cyclical process using user research to reach a final product. The patterns vary from product to product, and it is not always the same process pattern.

2. User Research

Card Sorting

Very rewarding in the user research process if applied well, card sorting can help establish the visual hierarchy of the interface prior to establishing the final hierarchy of menus, navigation, and information. Whether the purpose of the user research is to organize navigation in an app, game, website or to find the right audience for an application, this very simple method can proceed clearly onto the design process. There are three types of card sorting, as follows.

Open Cards

Users are given cards onto which they are tasked with writing categories (Figure 2.3), words, and sentences (UX matters 2016a). In addition, during the usability testing session, users may organize and write down categories and other tasks given during the session, beyond just sharing their opinions. With analog open cards, usually paper, pencils, and pens are used. This method is more effective in the early process of user testing because it may be done face to face with the user and the process can be effectively controlled and managed with more than one user at a time. This will vary according to the type of interface being tested (Figure 2.3).

The modified Delphi method (Figure 2.4), another open card method, helps create a participatory environment for a group of users—usually 8–10—testing the interface. A third option is online open card testing (Figure 2.5), which is very helpful if the researcher cannot be in the same place as the user. In addition, this method allows open cards to be used globally, which can be helpful if the interface would benefit from input from various parts of the world.

This analog open-card-sorting method does not require a large number of users for testing and is more direct for a small audience.

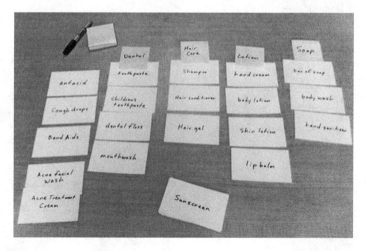

Figure 2.3

Analog open cards.

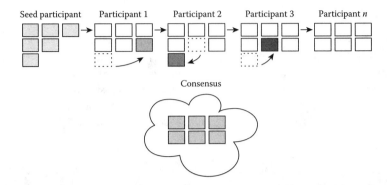

Figure 2.4

Example workflow of a modified Delphi method card-sorting study. (Courtesy of Paul, C. L., and Information Architecture Institute, A Modified Delphi Approach to New Card Sorting Methodology, *Journal of Usability Studies*, 2008;4(1):7–30.)

Figure 2.5

Online application for open cards. (Courtesy of UXmatters, http://www.uxmatters.com/mt/archives/2011/06/comparing-user-research-methods-for-information-architecture.php.)

Figure 2.6

Concept 7 and Pro Insight designed a study using closed cards, regarding how users interact with mobile and desktop devices. (Courtesy of Tobii Pro, http://www.tobiipro.com/fields-of-use/user-experience-interaction/customer-cases/concept7/.)

Closed Cards

In the closed cards method, users are extremely limited, to only a few steps. They may organize, answer specific questions, and perform any other limited task as assigned. Usually, this method takes less time than open cards testing (Figure 2.6).

Hybrid

Using a mix of open and closed cards in user testing sessions gives the user researcher greater assurance in some circumstances by recording more data. This is necessary only if the data are not clear.

Usually, testing users receive some type of payment or reward for their time and service. Sometimes the study can take more than one session. The user and the researcher need to come to an agreement regarding how much users will be paid for their time. A written, confidential agreement must be given to all users prior to testing. Sometimes, the arrangement might be voluntary, all depending on the project. Even when users volunteer, an agreement must be signed on behalf of both parties.

Card sorting can be done in person or with card-sorting software, even remotely over the Internet. There are various ways to apply the method, with no specific questions to ask or ways to organize studies. Each usability testing project must be different, according to the needs of the product and its users.

Each session should not extend longer than 20–60 minutes at a time, as users become exhausted. Because their brains need time to rest, after 60 minutes the results will be less fruitful than earlier parts of the session. A break or interruption every 10 minutes is suggested, because the brain gets exhausted and distracted, according to John Medina's research (Figure 2.7). Be aware that if sessions are aimed at children or elderly users, sessions might need to be as short as 5 minutes, depending on age.

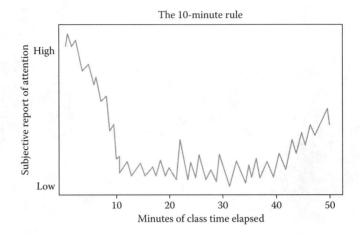

Figure 2.7

Medina, The 10-minute rule. Washington. (Courtesy of Brain Rules, http://www. brainrules.net/attention/?scene=1.)

Figure 2.8

User Testing paper prototypes in Afensol Elderly Home. (Courtesy of Copenhagen Institute of Interaction Design, Copenhagen, Denmark, http://ciid.dk/education/ portfolio/py/courses/graphical-user-interface/projects/happy-mail/.)

For more detailed analysis, a usability expert should be available to support and help as needed. In addition, it is necessary to observe and evaluate at least five people to obtain valid results; samples could be as large as 30, 100, or even more people, according to the project's budget and requirements (Figure 2.8).

Moreover, prior to any session, the researcher must decide whether to be present during the sessions as an evaluator or absent, which could affect the results.

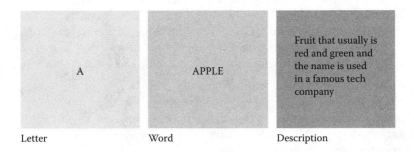

Letter	Word	Description
A	APPLE	Fruit that usually is red and green and the name is used in a famous tech company

Figure 2.9

Coleman, Letter, Word, and Description.

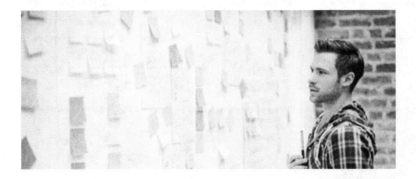

Figure 2.10

Paper color sorting. (Courtesy of Randall, A.S., 2016, UX Research Method Spotlight: Card Sorting.)

Sometimes, the presence of the tester negatively impacts the results, even causing a failure in observation. For example, some user testers might be tempted to ask questions of the researcher, which could distract or overinform the users being tested. Therefore, it is sometimes necessary to record a live video of the sessions so that an overall evaluation can occur after they are completed. Card sorting can be applied several times during the design process, and there are many types of evaluation (Figures 2.9 and 2.10). Each user testing is different. Many types of testing can only be used for one product, because each user testing demonstrates the need to revise and improve something in order to evolve the product to a higher level. The more intuitive the design becomes as a result of testing, the more successful the product will be in the end.

Graphical Steps

1. Hand out cards or begin using sorting card software, online or offline.
2. Give Task 1 to the user (timed by user researcher).
3. End of Task 1.
4. Give Task 2 to the user (timed by user researcher).

5. End of Task 3.
6. There may be more tasks. Once all tasks are done, everyone is given a reward for their time (money, food, etc.).
7. Testing session concludes.

Examples of Card Sorting Information Architecture

Card sorting can be extremely helpful when redesigning, creating, or editing an interface (Figures 2.11–2.14). It can create or help to create a new information architecture, navigational system, and overall content. In a way, card sorting is the root or structure of the entire user interface and should therefore be taken seriously from the beginning of the process.

There are many software packages available. Some are free for use over a limited time, some are open source, and some have a fee (Optimal Workshop 2016).

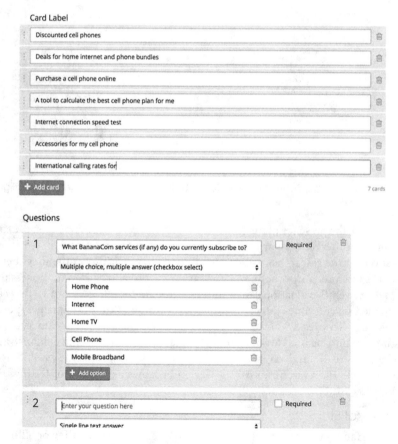

Figure 2.11

Card Sorting 101. Optimal Workshop, Wellington, New Zealand. (From Optimal Workshop, https://www.optimalworkshop.com/optimalsort.)

Figure 2.12

Individual card-sorting testing. (Courtesy of Serabox, 2016, http://serabox.com/
2012/03/refined-card-sort/.)

Figure 2.13

AnswerLab executing a card-sorting study with a group. (Courtesy of Basecamp, 2016,
https://signalvnoise.com/posts/2446-bootstrapped-profitable-proud-answerlab.)

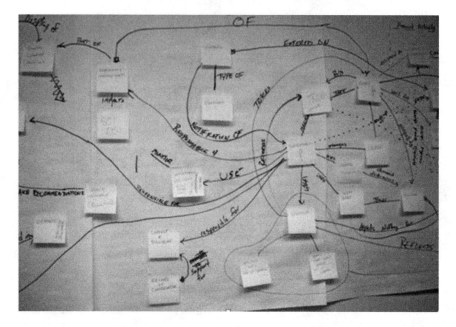

Figure 2.14

Various layers in card sorting using network connections. (Courtesy of Max Andriani, 2016, http://www.maxandriani.art.br/2012/11/20/card-sorting-uma-janela-para-a-mente/.)

Contextual Interviews

These are interviews done in an informal setting. Testing must be done in the most closed scenario, with the real user experience of the product. Such testing is very successful because the user feels comfortable, since the environment fits with the interface being tested. In addition, the user researcher can examine and gather data regarding the environment and its relationship to the user. The interview data collected are qualitative rather than quantitative.

Capital One, a bank, has created various locations across the United States combining a bank and a coffee shop (Figure 2.15). For example, if a user is struggling with a Capital One app or website, a Capital One employee can help. In addition, Capital One has launched a new group at the Capital One Labs (Figure 2.16) called *USERLabs* that comes to these coffee places to do informal interviews about their user interfaces. Overall, this is a great way for Capital One to revitalize its company continuously by welcoming its users in a friendly and relaxed environment while receiving feedback at the same time.

Figure 2.15

Capital One combined bank and coffee shop in Midtown Manhattan, New York. Photo by Jonathan Wiggs, Globe Staff. (Courtesy of *Boston Globe*, 2016, https://www.bostonglobe.com/business/2015/05/19/caffeine-and-banking-capital-one-cafe/EitGXUblPJZMet9fRwSBQM/story.html.)

Figure 2.16

Capital One Labs. (Courtesy of Capital One, NY, USA, 2016, https://www.capital-onelabs.com/images/about-background-slide.jpg.)

First-Click Testing

When testing the interaction of a user with an interface, first-click testing is very important. Whether with a mouse click, tap, or gesture, this step helps the researcher or designer to make a better interface. The percentage of users choosing the right place to click first is crucial, defining the success of the final product. A 90% positive click rate indicates future success for the interface (Gerry McGovern 2016). Every user wants intuitive navigation and access to information. Many users get frustrated within the first 30 seconds and never return. Therefore, creating a successful user experience for the first 90 seconds is very important.

For example, if a user wants to make a purchase online, they want to be done in minutes. The modern consumer lacks the patience to wait and finds it frustrating to be unable to find what they want. If they don't find what they want, they will close an app or website and look somewhere else. Overall, user experience is a time competition: how fast can a user access, retrieve, search, download, and view the information or product on offer. With many options out there in this competitive market, outstanding apps must be strong from the outset.

Overall, tracking time is essential and will vary with user age, maturity level, and level of experience with technology. All of these factors become part of the data collected during first-click testing.

Focus Group

In a focus group, users share their opinions about the service provided by the experience of the interface. Focus groups also help brainstorm ideas as a group to find better solutions than one user alone could find. The questions asked and the discussions must be friendly, open-ended, and flexible so that users feel comfortable sharing their true opinions.

Video or audio recordings of the focus group will help researchers gather more data later, if needed, without consulting the users again. It is also very helpful for someone to take notes during the session.

A written agreement must be secured before the focus group starts. Members of the focus group should provide explicit written permission for audio and video recording during the tests.

For later analysis, when organizing the group, it is important for the researcher to categorize users according to the following criteria:

1. Age.
2. Occupation.
3. Education.
4. Experience.
5. Gender.
6. Ethnicity.

7. Hobbies or anything else needed to help narrow the outcome of the focus group.
8. It may even be helpful for the study to ask users to write something about themselves to discover their character, their likes, and their dislikes.

Creating Personalities

The researcher must create personalities and define the character of each user, because greater information about each user allows the researcher to ask more direct questions, according to the purpose of usability testing. The personalities created may vary according to the needs of the study (RMS 2010). Sometimes, the user researcher may need global male and female perspectives, while another study may relate to women between 20 and 30 years old. Every study is different, no matter how many studies a user researcher has performed in the past (Department of Health and Human Services 2013a).

Heuristics for User Interface Design

Heuristic Evaluation/Expert Review

Heuristic evaluation is used to locate problems with the interface without testing and may be applied at any time during the process, as needed (Department of Health and Human Services 2013b). The issues the user, researcher, designer, or programmer finds will vary according to their points of view. Reviews may be informal to facilitate the design of the interface and functionality. For further information on this topic, see Chapter 12 (Tognazzini 2014).

Nielsen's heuristics (Nielsen 2016a, 2016b) from 1994 suggests many factors to consider when evaluating an interface:

1. *Visibility of System Status*—Do the functions of the interface look readable?
2. *Match between System and the Real World*—The visual system should be intuitive and easy to understand for anyone observing the interface.
3. *User Control and Freedom*—The interface must present information clearly, while avoiding dialog boxes.
4. *Consistency and Standards*—The interface must be consistent throughout the design and agree with current standards regarding icons, design principles, and user-centered visual design.
5. *Error Prevention*—Avoiding error messages is the best way to make sure an interface works perfectly.
6. *Recognition Rather Than Recall*—The user should be able to navigate without the need to remember; everything should be intuitive and easily accessible, without making the system complex.
7. *Flexibility and Efficiency of Use*—Accelerators try to find a balance between novice and expert users. The interface should be as easy for a novice to interact with as for an expert user.

8. *Esthetic and Minimalist Design*—User interfaces should follow visual design guidelines; there should be nothing extra or superfluous within the interface. A successful design esthetic is easy to access and minimalist in every way. Only what is needed visually should be there.

9. *Help Users Recognize, Diagnose, and Recover from Errors*—Any error message should be clear to the user and present a way to resolve the problem constructively so that the user feels safe and confident about the product.

10. *Help and Documentation*—It is better for an interface to have no need for documentation, help, or tutorials, but these may be required in large systems that have many in-depth, complex, and layered functions that may not be easily displayed to the eye all at once.

Individual Interviews

This type of user research allows a more in-depth analysis of any product. Interviews usually last 20 minutes to an hour, depending on the number of questions that the interviewer has to ask the user.

Quite like focus groups, the interviews can happen physically face to face, online through video chat, over email, or by phone conference. The researcher needs to make a decision about which format would be best for the product.

Sometimes, when there is a need to evaluate a large number of users, it may be best to do online surveys, which are explained later in this chapter. Individual interviews can become time-consuming if not arranged properly, and the resulting data could be insufficient if fewer than five people are interviewed. Even more may be needed depending on the research.

Parallel Design

This research method is very important in the interface design stage if a company has several designers, because they may come with their own design ideas. Evaluation criteria are needed, and then different ideas can be shared in a group discussion. During this discussion, designers grab ideas from each concept and blend them into a new, stronger concept. In this way, the interface becomes successful and ready for user testing (Figure 2.17).

Sometimes, parallel design examinations can be applied multiple times to advance the design of the project. For example, designers may use this method in sketches, a low-fidelity prototype, and a high-fidelity prototype. Some companies make this method into a competition, which is incorrect; designers should be working together toward one good cause, to resolve the user's problem.

Personas

Usually, a user researcher needs to narrow the audience by evaluating which personas will be interacting with the product. The wider the audience, the more user

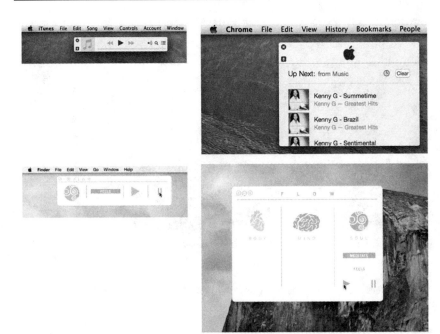

Figure 2.17

Comparison of two digital prototypes: iTunes on the top and Flow on the bottom. Both apps have a similar purpose; Flow caters to an audience with a more balanced lifestyle.

Steve Medeiros
"My parents taught me not to talk to strangers."

- Age: 22
- Role: Graduate
- Area: Finance
- Computer Literacy: High

- Recent graduate of Syracuse University
- Accepted a job in NYC
- Bored of his routine, looking for something new

Figure 2.18

Persona example. (Courtesy of UX Booth, 2016, http://assets.uxbooth.com/uploads/2011/08/image1.png.)

research is required. When evaluating a persona, not only the persona's environment but also his or her personal, professional, and technical background and motivation are analyzed (Figures 2.18 and 2.19). This method answers specific questions, providing very specific goals and benefits to user research (Goodwin et al. 2016).

Figure 2.19

Persona study by Frog Design. (Courtesy of Vimeo, 2016, https://vimeo.com/72911626.)

Example of a Profile of a Person

- Be aware.
- Is this the right feel and experience for the persona?
- Do not concentrate on the user's favorite font or color.

To organize persona information, consider the examples below:

1. *Narrative:* Personas with more in-depth information.
2. *Table:* Personas with a medium amount of information.
3. *The quick and dirty:* Personas with a small amount of information.

This evaluation not only helps narrow down the users but also strengthens the product branding from the early stages.

Prototyping

Though a method applied in the design field, our job as visual interface designers is to create the prototype. Without a prototype, there can be no advancement or progress in the project's user research. Prototyping is thus important from beginning to end.

This book has an entire chapter on prototyping (see Chapter 3). There are two overall types.

Low Fidelity

Such prototypes are usually done on paper (Figure 2.20).

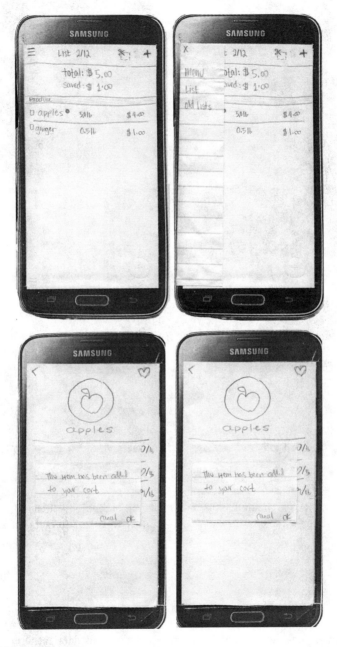

Figure 2.20

Shopping app by Mariko Sakemi, low-fidelity prototype.

Figure 2.21

Shopping app by Mariko Sakemi, high-fidelity prototype.

High Fidelity

These prototypes are usually done using current technology, through which the prototype has the look and feel of a final product and also interacts with the user (Figure 2.21).

Online Surveys

Online surveys are very helpful when the user researcher has a small set of specific questions and wants to narrow down the research choices. A trained expert must analyze the content and analyze the final data gathered from all surveys.

Below are some sample questions used in online surveys. These are only examples; nobody should feel compelled to use these questions. They are meant as inspiration that may help you devise better questions geared to your specific product.

1. Are you (the user) able to find the information or function you seek?
2. Are you satisfied with the interface?
3. Have you had similar experiences with other interfaces?
4. What do you like about the interface?
5. What do you dislike about the interface?
6. Do you find any functions or information on the interface frustrating?
7. Do you know of any other interfaces that do a better job than this interface?
8. Do you have any suggestions or ideas to improve the interface?
9. If this concept seems poor or does not relate to you, then please tell us about your interests. (Make sure the user never feels rejected.)

System Usability Scale

Created by John Brooke in 1986, the system usability scale (SUS) allows the evaluation of a wide range of products and services (University of Geneva 2016a). Again, this is an example; for user research, the SUS could change and be adapted to a different context. The scale shown in this example is very effective and makes it easy to collect data specifically from a large number of user testers (Figure 2.22).

Task Analysis

These days, task analysis is becoming increasingly important as we move away from the personal computer and toward small laptops, tablets, mobiles, and wearable interfaces. This testing is crucial for understanding user needs. For example, when walking down the street checking email, users want to be able to read or even respond while still walking. All the tasks possible when checking email must be evaluated for a user both in motion and at rest. Is the user able to write an email? Importantly, type legibility and the layout of the design must fulfill their functions. Analyzing use in various scenarios helps the user researcher, interface designer, and developer create a more efficient interface (Figure 2.23).

Task analysis, a field in its own right, is a very helpful tool for refining an interface and for finding and evaluating the feasibility of the user's main purpose. The user experience can be tested well within an environment, for personal use, and in global and cultural contexts (Hackos and Redish 1998; University of Geneva 2016b). Overall, task analysis facilitates a smoother interface experience.

System usability scale

© Digital Equipment Corporation, 1986.

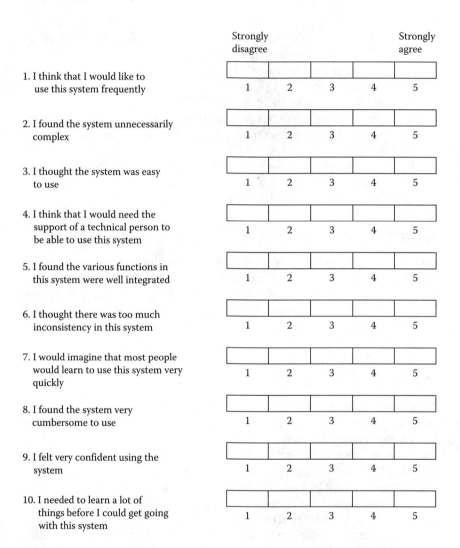

	Strongly disagree				Strongly agree
1. I think that I would like to use this system frequently	1	2	3	4	5
2. I found the system unnecessarily complex	1	2	3	4	5
3. I thought the system was easy to use	1	2	3	4	5
4. I think that I would need the support of a technical person to be able to use this system	1	2	3	4	5
5. I found the various functions in this system were well integrated	1	2	3	4	5
6. I thought there was too much inconsistency in this system	1	2	3	4	5
7. I would imagine that most people would learn to use this system very quickly	1	2	3	4	5
8. I found the system very cumbersome to use	1	2	3	4	5
9. I felt very confident using the system	1	2	3	4	5
10. I needed to learn a lot of things before I could get going with this system	1	2	3	4	5

Figure 2.22

System usability scale created by John Brooke. (Courtesy of University of Geneva, Geneva, Switzerland 2016b, http://cui.unige.ch/isi/icle-wiki/_media/ipm:test-suschapt.pdf.)

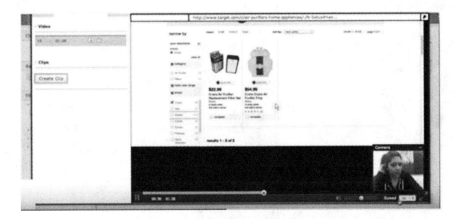

Figure 2.23

Using the user testing application userzoom.com, the woman on camera is evaluating how the products are located on the page and whether they seem visible or not when the user wants to select one and get more information about it. In this task, the user researcher is recording the user test through audio and video, which will prove very helpful for later or further analysis.

Use Cases

How to Write a Use Case

Write the steps of a use case in an easy-to-understand narrative.

Kenworthy (1997) outlines the following steps:

1. Identify who is going to be using the website.
2. Pick one of those users.
3. Define what that user wants to do on the site. Each thing the user does on the site becomes a use case.
4. For each use case, decide on the normal course of events followed.
5. Describe a basic course of events in the description of the use case. Describe the events in terms of what the user does and how the system responds in a way of which the user should be aware.
6. Once the basic course has been described, consider alternate courses of events and add those to "extend" the use case.
7. Look for commonalities among use cases. Extract these and note them as common course use cases.
8. Repeat Steps 2–7 for all other users.

Sample Use Cases

Consider Figure 2.24 of how to access the software user interface of an ATM machine:

Simple diagrams like Figure 2.24 show how to test an interface step-by-step in a clear and organized manner.

Main success scenario	Step	Description
	1	A: Inserts card
	2	S: Validates card and asks for PIN
A: Actor	3	A: Enters PIN
S : System	4	S: Validates PIN
	5	S: Allows access to account
Extensions	2a	Card not valid S: Displays message and rejects card
	4a	PIN not valid S: Displays message and asks for re-try (twice)
	4b	PIN invalid three times S: Eats card and exits

Figure 2.24

Steps for ATM access through PIN entry.

Usability Testing

Usability testing is essential to the research process. For more in-depth information, see Chapter 11.

References

Basecamp. Bootstrapped, Profitable, & Proud: AnswerLab. 2016. *Signal v. Noise by Basecamp.* Accessed July 30, 2016. https://signalvnoise.com/posts/2446-bootstrapped-profitable-proud-answerlab.

Boston Globe. Caffeine and Banking at Capital One 360 Cafe—The Boston Globe. 2016. *BostonGlobe.com.* Accessed July 30, 2016. https://www.bostonglobe.com/business/2015/05/19/caffeine-and-banking-capital-one-cafe/EitGXUblPJZMet9fRwSBQM/story.html.

Brain Rules. http://www.brainrules.net/, January. 2016. Attention | Brain Rules |. Accessed July 30, 2016. http://www.brainrules.net/attention/?scene=1.

Capital One Labs. 2016. Accessed July 30, 2016. https://www.capitalonelabs.com/images/about-background-slide.jpg.

CIID. Copenhagen Institute of Interaction Design. Happy Mail. 2016. Accessed July 30, 2016. http://ciid.dk/education/portfolio/py/courses/graphical-user-interface/projects/happy-mail/.

Department of Health and Human Services. 2013a. Focus Groups, June. Department of Health and Human Services. Accessed April 21, 2017. http://www.usability.gov/how-to-and-tools/methods/focus-groups.html.

Department of Health and Human Services. 2013b. Heuristic Evaluations and Expert Reviews, October. Department of Health and Human Services. Accessed April 21, 2017. http://www.usability.gov/how-to-and-tools/methods/heuristic-evaluation.html.

Gerry McGovern. The Vital Importance of the First Click | Gerry McGovern. 2016. Accessed July 30, 2016. http://www.gerrymcgovern.com/new-thinking/vital-importance-first-click.

Goodwin, Kim, Chris Calabrese, Cameron Winchester, and Shahrzad Samadzadeh (editors). 2016. *Perfecting Your Personas | Cooper Journal*. Accessed July 30, 2016. http://www.cooper.com/journal/2001/08/perfecting_your_personas.

Hackos, Joann T., and Janice C. Redish. 1998. *User and Task Analysis for Interface Design*. Wiley, Canada.

Max Andriani. *Card Sorting*: Uma Janela Para a Mente—Max Andriani | UX Designer. 2016. Accessed July 30, 2016. http://www.maxandriani.art.br/2012/11/20/card-sorting-uma-janela-para-a-mente/.

Moray, Neville. 2005. *Ergonomics: The History and Scope of Human Factors*. Taylor & Francis, New York.

Nielsen, Jakob. 2016a. Usability Inspection Methods. Accessed July 30, 2016. http://www.nngroup.com/books/usability-inspection-methods/.

Nielsen, Jakob. 2016b. 10 Heuristics for User Interface Design. Accessed July 30, 2016. http://www.nngroup.com/articles/ten-usability-heuristics/.

Optimal Workshop. 2016. Card Sorting Software | Optimal Workshop. Accessed July 30, 2016. https://www.optimalworkshop.com/optimalsort.

Paul, Celeste Lyn, and Information Architecture Institute. 2007. *A Modified Delphi Approach to a New Card Sorting Methodology*, JUS Journal of Usability Studies, Bloomingdale, IL.

Randall, Angela Schmeidel. 2016. UX Research Method Spotlight: Card Sorting. Accessed July 30, 2016. http://blog.normalmodes.com/when-to-outsource-usability-testing-0.

RMS. Focus Group Moderator Tips to Handle 7 Unique Personalities. 2010. *The Research Bunker*. August 20. Accessed April 21, 2017. https://rmsbunker-blog.wordpress.com/2010/08/20/focus-group-moderator-tips-to-handle-7-unique-personalities-focus-group-facility-in-watertown-ny-northern-ny/.

SeraBox. Refined Card Sort | Sera Koo. 2016. Accessed July 30, 2016. http://serabox.com/2012/03/refined-card-sort/.

Tobii Pro. Concept7. 2015. Accessed April 21, 2017. http://www.tobiipro.com/fields-of-use/user-experience-interaction/customer-cases/concept7/.

Tognazzini, Bruce. 2014. First Principles of Interaction Design (Revised & Expanded). *askTog*. March 6. Accessed April 21, 2017. http://asktog.com/atc/principles-of-interaction-design/.

University of Geneva. 2016a. Accessed July 30, 2016. http://cui.unige.ch/isi/icle-wiki/_media/ipm:test-suschapt.pdf.

University of Geneva. 2016b. Accessed July 30, 2016. http://cui.unige.ch/isi/icle-wiki/_media/ipm:test-suschapt.pdf.

UX Booth. 2016. Accessed July 30, 2016. http://assets.uxbooth.com/uploads/2011/08/ image1.png.

UX matters. Comparing User Research Methods for Information Architecture: UXmatters. 2016a. Accessed July 30, 2016. http://www.uxmatters.com/ mt/archives/2011/06/comparing-user-research-methods-for-information-architecture.php.

UX matters. Comparing User Research Methods for Information Architecture: UXmatters. 2016b. Accessed July 30, 2016. http://www.uxmatters.com/ mt/archives/2011/06/comparing-user-research-methods-for-information-architecture.php.

Vimeo. *Aging in Place: Part Two.* 2016. Accessed July 30, 2016. https://vimeo. com/72911626.

3

Early Stages of User Experience and Prototyping

How Do You Start Prototyping?

Prototyping an interface takes place in various stages.

Where to Start

The earliest stage of prototyping involves making a quick sketch of thoughts and ideas on a piece of paper, board, tablet, or napkin. The surface does not matter. As long as the designer or concept designer starts putting the ideas together somewhere, it will help him or her move to the next step. At this stage, the designer is usually not ready to show the sketch to anyone else because it is probably too abstract for someone else to understand. All visual designers, not only those in the field of interface design, get their ideas down one way or another, like a seed in the ground, ready to grow. It is important to keep a sketchbook or another place where you can brainstorm your ideas. If you choose to use paper, I encourage you to buy a sketchbook. If you are more technologically oriented and prefer to work on a tablet or laptop, I encourage you to get an application that allows you to sketch and save.

Sketching

The sketching process looks different if done individually or as a team. If done individually, you need to have a sketchbook or a notebook in which you can write down your ideas and brainstorm. Ideas may come in words, images, or diagrams. As long as you understand your early sketches, you will be able to refine your sketches and share the revised versions with your team or client. If sketching is done as a team, you will probably place a large piece of paper on the wall, brainstorming first by creating a mind map and then later starting to organize the user interface (UI) by using sticky notes, making it easy to move things around if anything is changed (Figure 3.1).

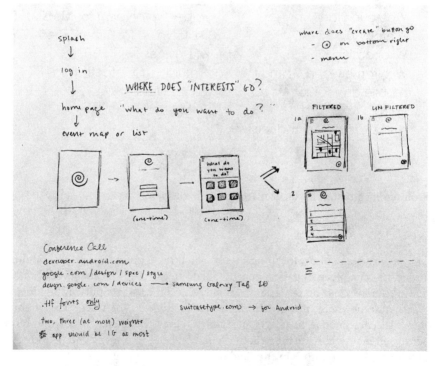

Figure 3.1

Sketching wireframes in a sketchbook including images, words, and sentences for a user interface prototype by Carmella Pombuena and Lloyd Paolo Prudente.

Choosing the Right Sketchbook

Sketchbooks are sold online or in any art supply store such as Utrecht or Michaels. Of the many types of sketchbooks, I suggest you to choose one of the following (Figure 3.2):

1. Moleskine sketchbook
2. Responsive Design sketchbook
3. Dot Grid Book sketchbook
4. UI Stencils pocket sketchbook
5. UI Stencils sketch pad
6. Any other sketchbook that you may prefer to work with

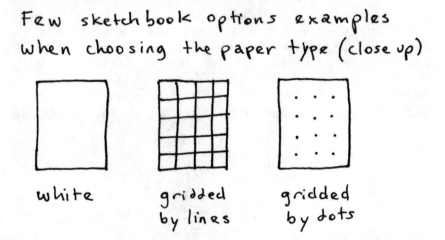

Few sketch book options examples when choosing the paper type (close up)

white   gridded by lines   gridded by dots

Figure 3.2

Of the various types of sketchbook backgrounds, these are recommended for brainstorming, sketching, wireframing, and creating workflows.

Choosing Other Helpful Tools

1. Pentel p207 Drafting Pencil, or any other pencil that you prefer.
2. Sharpies (you will find yourself using some thicknesses more than others, depending on their purpose) will really help you create hierarchy throughout the process. The options are Ultra Fine Point, Fine Point, Retractable, Twin Tip, and Chisel Tip.
3. Opaque gray markers.
4. Color markers.
5. Eraser.
6. Pixel ruler.
7. Android stencil (if creating for Android).

Overall, the early sketching process of prototyping is quick due to its low fidelity, which makes it faster to place ideas down and change and move things around. In addition, for designers who do not like working on paper, smart boards are a great option, because you can move words and images around and edit them, and the result is saved as a digital image that you can share. Another personal option is any tablet device that has a pen or stylus, which can help you quickly write down your ideas.

Mind maps (Figures 3.5 through 3.7) are helpful for organizing information as well as creating hierarchy and the personality of the interface. You can create mind maps alone or in a group. They are the fastest way to get ideas out, not only for UI design but also for solving other types of problems in various fields dealing with organization.

Paul Baran's network models (1964; Figure 3.3) are great examples of ways of connecting visually. Though Paul Baran created these network types for the communications technology of that time, they can still be applied visually in mind maps when diagramming ideas. If applied from a visual perspective, the centralized model is when everything connects to one main concept, in which case there are only two levels of hierarchy. The first level, in the center, is where all lines connect, while the second level is all the lines connecting to that center. The decentralized model is a way to create various groups, each with something

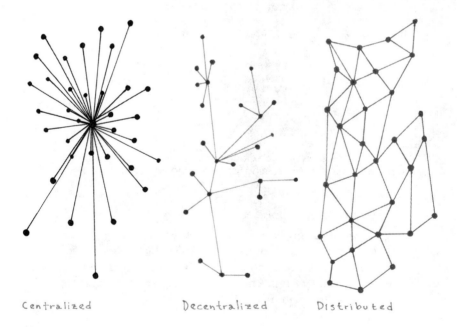

Centralized   Decentralized   Distributed

Figure 3.3

Paul Baran's network models (1964).

that has the first level of importance, while there are lines of the second or third level of importance connecting to the first level. The levels of hierarchy could also extend beyond two or three in depth. Meanwhile, the distributed model can have various levels of hierarchy, with all points relating and having some connection to the other ideas.

Figure 3.4 presents various network topologies, ways of connecting networks, which can all be applied to our diagram thinking process. These are ring, mesh, star, fully connected, tree, line, and bus. If you have created mind maps and diagrams, you have probably already created one of the examples above without thinking.

Sketching is the *most important* part of the UI process. Once you are through with sketching, you *cannot* turn back, especially if your prototype has become high fidelity, meaning it has already been programmed with a prototyping tool. If the project returns to sketching at any point, it is going back to the beginning, resulting in a lost investment in time and money for the client. It is best to get *all ideas* and *solutions* out during the sketching process so you can *revise mistakes* quickly.

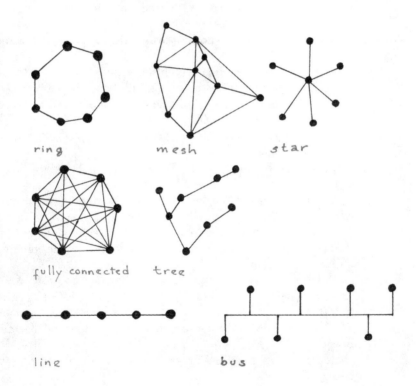

Figure 3.4

Network topologies.

As mentioned earlier, there are many ways to get your ideas out there. Mind mapping is just one. Below is an easy classification of ways of brainstorming created by Turi McKinley from Frog Design:

1. Journey mapping (in general stages from beginning to end, also known as *lateral thinking*, which is a term coined by Edward de Bono; for more information, visit http://www.debonothinkingsystems.com/tools/lateral.htm). A video example can be found at http://vimeo.com/72911626.

2. Concepting (groups of people should feel free to share ideas without judgement, which opens the path to ideas or concepts) and prototyping.

3. List created originally by Frog with Turi McKinley is below:
   a. List clients' needs. (Organize by priority and ask if the client has examples of other UIs from competitors. How can we improve the current market compared with other, similar businesses?)
   b. Diagramming purpose or the purposes of the UI. (Menus, functions, solutions, problems, outcomes.) Journey mapping: concepting and prototyping.
   c. Is this doable within the budget? (Possibilities are more open with a larger budget.)
   d. How can the interface solve the problem proposed?
   e. Users need fast and intuitive access. (Think about how many screens or pages are needed in the UI to obtain the required functionality.) How are we solving this problem?
   f. Does the interface need its own personalized icons? What about typography? (Take notes!)
   g. How will the branding of the UI embody the branding of the company?
   h. Is this a new company, and does it need its own branding or a logo as well?
   i. Think about a color system. Write down color options, and analyze the meaning and symbolism behind each color used in the branding, if there is more than one.
   j. Start sketching a layout by using all the information above.
   k. Ask your client for a copy of the content for the UI. Copywriting for UI is very different than for books or manuals, for example. The writing needs to be consistent, simple, understandable, and brief.
   l. Share your earlier organized and revised sketches of the UI with your client(s).

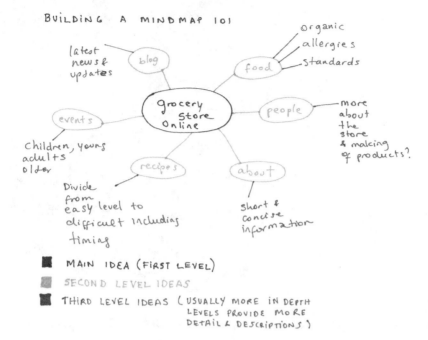

Figure 3.5

Building a mind map sketch to create and organize an online grocery store. In this example, there are three levels.

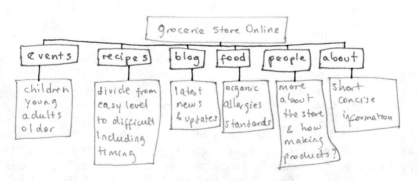

Figure 3.6

Organizing the hierarchy of the content of an online grocery store through a tree diagram.

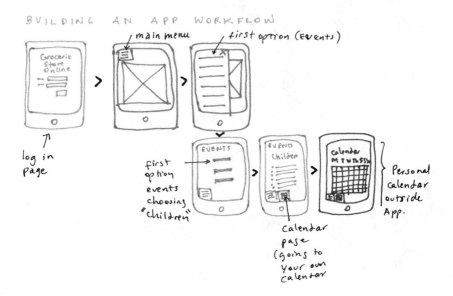

Figure 3.7

Creating the workflow of an app through rapid sketching.

More Options and Types of Tools

Low-fidelity prototypes should be close to or the actual size. This type of prototype is also called *wireframing*, because the designer begins to create a more structural version of the idea created in the brainstorming and mind-mapping step.

1. Pencil
2. Pens and paper (heavy, medium, and light weights)
3. Scissors
4. Glue
5. Reusable adhesive tape
6. X-Acto knife
7. Cutting mat
8. Pixel ruler
9. Video recording (to record the experience of the user with the UI)

When recording interactivity, a user rather than the designer must test the prototype, even at an early stage. The user should be involved in all stages, from beginning to end. Reward the user, and do not put pressure on him or her while he or she interacts with the UI. Users will give you feedback about whether they understand the functionality, whether they find it easy to interact with the interface, or whether some things need to be fixed. In addition, find someone to test the prototype UI who fits its audience. If your user audience is broad, finding someone will be easy. But if your audience is narrow, for example, if the UI is only for children aged 4–7 years, you definitely need to find a user to test who fits that type.

3. Early Stages of User Experience and Prototyping

Wireframing

Wireframing is a fast way to organize a layout by using paper and pencil or wireframing software. The layout of a website or app will vary according to the content and user's needs. This step helps us begin to have a clearer idea of where the project is going, because we begin to think not only about where the navigation and content should be presented but also about the branding, including colors and typefaces, that should be applied to the app or website we are creating. You can also take notes and write around the wireframe. Even though it is a rough version of the finished product, it is essential to create several versions of the layout before finally making a decision. Chapter 8 explains the layout and grid in depth, which are essential for the structure of the layout.

Skipping wireframing can be dangerous for future steps, because at this step decisions are made about the structure and how the app or website will stand. Just as an architect cannot build a house without a blueprint, a designer cannot build an app or website without a wireframe. Wireframes range from rough to one prepared digitally and later printed. Regardless of the method adopted, what matters is to solve the problem and make the app or website accessible to and friendly for the user.

Wireframes for a Game for Mobile and Tablet

This wireframe shows a layout on a tablet, with space for a description at the bottom. The tablet background was already created prior to sketching. It is recommended to create layouts digitally, which sizes the design area more precisely and shortens the time needed for sketching. If you create a background template similar to the one in this example, you can easily print 100 of them to draw on. In addition, many templates are available online for various devices, for purchase or for free.

In this example, in order to create a better wireframe, the interface designer chose to print a piece of paper with the color of the intended background. In this case, the wireframe is geared toward tablets. The Hex app is a game geared toward the elderly (Figure 3.8). The game has several levels. These examples show Levels 1, 2, 3, and 4 (Figures 3.9 and 3.10).

Movement in the game is performed along diagonals that have been set up by the game.

Paper Prototyping

This step is a fast and easy way to prototype an app or website at low cost without programming or development, while still allowing users to test the prototype. The UI designer can use the same tools as described above for the sketching process, using an X-Acto knife or scissors, glue, tape, sticky notes, and even cardboard to

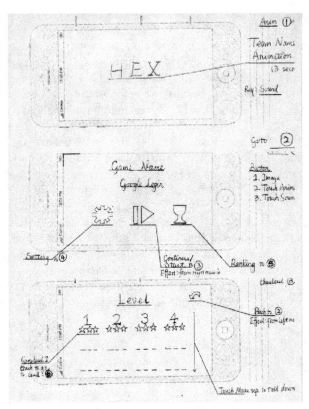

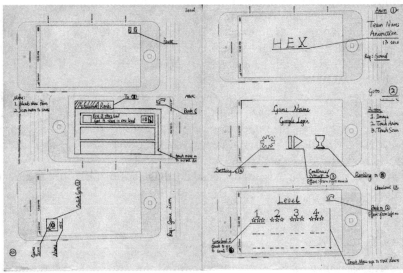

Figure 3.8

Wireframing of the Hex app, created by Elsie Nolasco.

3. Early Stages of User Experience and Prototyping

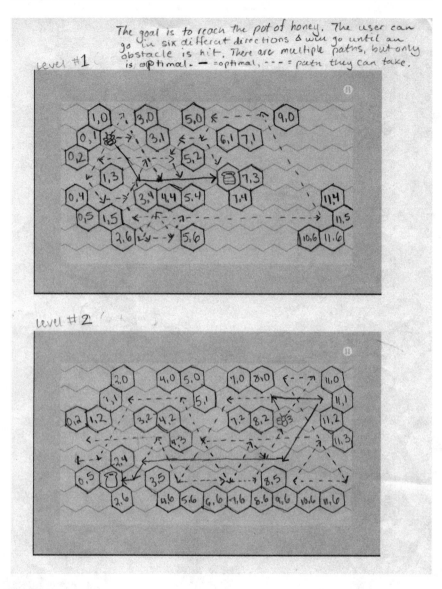

Figure 3.9

Wireframing of the Hex app, Stage 2 organizing, Levels 1 and 2.

create a simulation the size of the device. In the prototyping stage, we can make corrections in seconds, redrawing the layout or anything else needed. In addition, the prototype provides users with multidimensional access, allowing them to interact with their own gestures and the app or website's levels of hierarchy. Overall, prototyping is essential for the process of creating a UI.

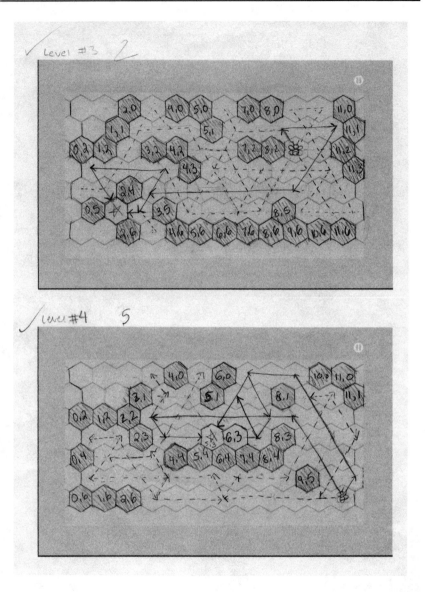

Figure 3.10

Wireframing of the Hex app, Stage 2, Levels 3 and 4.

User Experience and Testing

The paper prototype gives users access to an early-stage app or website project. User experience must be implemented early in the process, not only at the end. Many companies invest millions of dollars to revamp the user experience of their products. In this competitive market, with banks adding coffee restaurants, the

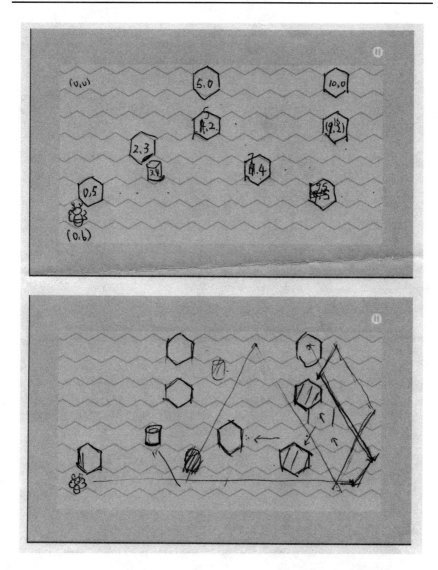

Figure 3.11

Sketches of the structure of movement and around the space in the Hex app.

social app designs created by various products, and companies connecting various types of cultures through the promotion of their products, the user experience is like water to the growing plant that is the product. Without feedback, the UI designer cannot know if he or she has found the best solution. Even at this stage, it is important to run tests and apply in detail the user research carried out for the project (Figures 3.11 and 3.12). Read more about user research in Chapter 2, and for further information about testing, see Chapter 13.

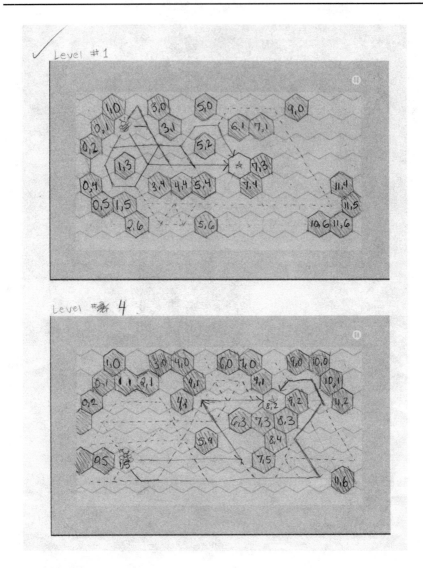

Figure 3.12

Sketches of the structure of the points gained during the game, Hex app.

Paper Prototyping for Mobile

In this example, the interface designer shows an app that helps the user choose the right combination of colors. The paper prototype shows a cutout form of a smartphone. The prototype screen may be easily adjusted by placing cutouts representing different stages of the process of using the application, from choosing a color to emailing the color combinations (Figure 3.13). This type of prototyping can be also carried out by using pen and paper.

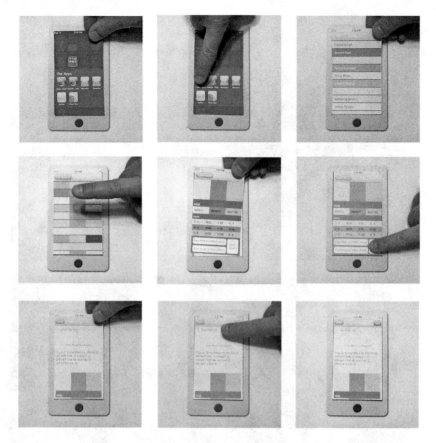

Figure 3.13

Prototyping with digitally printed wireframing. (Courtesy of YouTube, 2011, https://www.youtube.com/watch?v=V8LNDqMlapY.)

Prototyping for Other Types of Devices

Figure 3.14 shows the process of using the blood-analysis interface, including entering the first screen, paying for the service by cash or credit card, and sharing the results right after blood is taken from one of the user's fingers.

The FriendlyAnimals application is geared toward children. Figure 3.15 shows the process of entering the FriendlyAnimals interface and interacting with the coloring page section.

The example above shows only a few of the options available when creating paper prototypes. There are a thousand ways of creating low-fidelity prototypes, depending on the specific UI interface and hardware. For example, an interface for Google Glass or another wearable interface will require a different approach to creating low-fidelity prototypes. The prototype UI is based on the creativity of the UI designer(s) assigned to the project, with every UI prototype varying

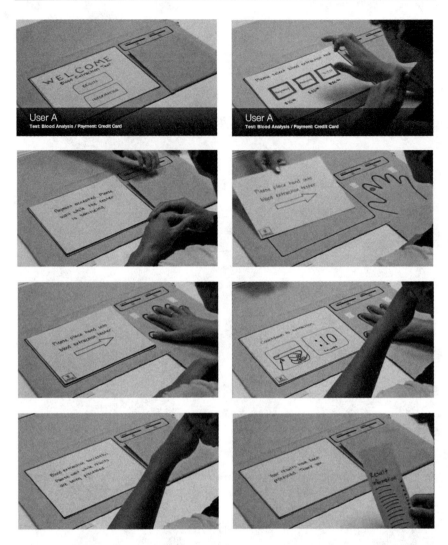

Figure 3.14

Paper prototyping for a blood-analysis application. (Courtesy of YouTube, 2009, https://www.youtube.com/watch?v=_g4GGtJ8NCY.)

according to the interface's purpose. Understanding, responding to, and finding solutions to users' needs are important when working on the paper prototype.

However, UI design cannot solely rely on creativity. The interface designer must be aware of the limitations placed on sizes by screens, images, icons, and much more. It is important to remain in constant contact with the development team during this early process. A wide range of devices requires UIs, including smartphones, tablets, watches (wearables), TVs, automobiles, and much more.

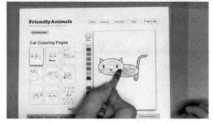

Figure 3.15

Paper prototyping for desktop. (Courtesy of YouTube, 2010, https://www.youtube.com/watch?v=9wQkLthhHKA.)

Follow interface standards and guidelines in your design. The Apple, Android, and Windows guidelines are provided here as an example.

Apple Human Interface Guidelines: https://developer.apple.com/ios/human-interface-guidelines/

Android Design: https://developer.android.com/design/handhelds/index.html

Windows: https://developer.microsoft.com/en-us/windows/design

For further and more developed examples, see Chapters 14 through 16.

Simulating Interactivity in Paper Prototyping

When creating prototypes, it is important to represent some type of interactivity, such as linking, search, and pop-up windows. There are many ways to create this interaction through layers that overlap the prototype with the change compared with the previous function. In addition, you can use highlighters, markers of various colors, or colored paper. The tools you use do not matter, as long as you get the point across to the user during direct testing.

Designing the user experience begins with visualizing the identity of the app and creating a skeleton or structure for the interactivity: create and add icons, windows, menus, and many other design patterns, as needed. It is very important to fix all errors during this stage. A paper prototype without a user experience is not a paper UI prototype.

Helpful tips for early prototypes:

1. When you test the prototype, do not tell the user what to do, which takes away the user's intuitive response to the interface.
2. Allow the user to take their time when interacting with the prototype.
3. Take notes on any suggestions or improvements the user makes.
4. Take notes of positive feedback as well!
5. If you have any doubts about certain functions, this is the time to ask the user for his or her thoughts on those aspects of the prototype.

For further in-depth information about usability testing and acceptance, see Chapter 13, which explains how to get results and provides other helpful steps. In addition, it is important for the designer to learn more about patterns during this process. Chapter 7 has further information in that regard. Patterns should also be applied in the early process of prototyping (Barth 2013; Beetem, n.d.; Bjelland and Kristian, n.d.; Buxton 2010; Greenberg et al. 2012; Saffer 2008; Sinha and Landay 2001; Christensen and Kreplin 1984).

References

Barth, Jan. 2013. *Prototyping Interfaces: Interaktives Skizzieren Mit Vvvv*, Schmidt-Friderichs GmbH, Mainz, Germany.

Beetem, J. F. n.d. Visualizing Optimization Algorithms via Rapid Prototyping of Graphical User Interfaces. In *[1992 Proceedings] The Third International Workshop on Rapid System Prototyping*. doi:10.1109/iwrsp.1992.243900, North Carolina.

Bjelland, Hans V., and Tangeland Kristian. n.d. User-Centered Design Proposals for Prototyping Haptic User Interfaces. In *Lecture Notes in Computer Science*, pp. 110–20, Springer, Berlin, Heidelberg.

Buxton, Bill. 2010. *Sketching User Experiences: Getting the Design Right and the Right Design*. Morgan Kaufmann, San Francisco, CA.

Christensen, Niels, and Kreplin, Klaus-Dieter. 1984. Prototyping of User-Interfaces. In *Approaches to Prototyping*, pp. 58–67, Springer, F.R. Germany.

Greenberg, Saul, Sheelagh Carpendale, Bill Buxton, and Nicolai Marquardt. 2012. *Sketching User Experiences*. Elsevier, Waltham, MA.

Saffer, Dan. 2008. *Designing Gestural Interfaces: Touchscreens and Interactive Devices*. O'Reilly Media, Inc. Sebastopol, CA.

Sinha, Anoop K., and James A. Landay. 2001. Visually Prototyping Perceptual User Interfaces through Multimodal Storyboarding. In *Proceedings of the 2001 Workshop on Perceptive User Interfaces—PUI '01*. doi:10.1145/971478.971501.

YouTube. *Example Usability Test with a Paper Prototype.* 2010. Accessed April 21, 2017. https://www.youtube.com/watch?v=9wQkLthhHKA.

YouTube. *iPhone User Interface Design, Paper Prototype Study.* 2011. Accessed April 21, 2017. https://www.youtube.com/watch?v=V8LNDqMIapY.

YouTube. *Paper Prototyping.* 2009. Accessed April 21, 2017. https://www.youtube.com/watch?v=_g4GGtJ8NCY.

SECTION II
Design

4

Psychology of Color

Introduction

Color is part of our daily routine, from our waking life and imagination to our dreams. The meaning of color starts from our general perspective. For example, the sun is yellow, which we know without thinking. We have seen the sun so many times that it is part of our subconscious minds. But the meaning of yellow in our dreams is an entirely different answer; each person will react to yellow from a different perspective. Do they have a fear of yellow, or perhaps a negative or positive association with it? In this case, the meaning of yellow will vary from individual to individual.

We do not discuss in depth how to understand color's various levels and types of meaning. Instead, we analyze the human visual experience solely in the context of interaction with interfaces. We cannot classify and define all colors, because everyone has a different relationship to color based on past experience. Therefore, we consider the basics of color and their general meanings, which may vary according by country and culture.

Considered psychologically, color is a nonvocal, purely visual means of communication. In design, color is similar to typefaces. How you use color—darker or lighter—creates a personality that complements the content, including the images and typography. The color or colors used speak to the user just as much as the type itself. It is important to make a decision early in your project about what color or colors to use in the interface, because without color the interface would be incomplete.

Brain Stimulation

The use of color creates different dimensions of depth within the hierarchy and identity of the UI. The user not only accesses information but also receives subconscious and psychological messages from the colors in the UI that are related specifically to the user.

Each type of color stimulates different parts of our brain, such as the following:

1. Anger
2. Hunger
3. Happiness
4. Worry
5. Fatigue
6. Excitement
7. Concentration

Swiss psychologist Carl Jung identified four color energies that define our temperaments: cool blue, earth green, sunshine yellow, and fiery red ("Can Color Really Change How You Feel and Act?" 2016). Everyone has characteristics of all these colors, but some people have less of some colors and more of others. Therefore, there is no perfect equation defining universal color psychology, but the characteristics may be used to keep testing ("Can Color Really Change How You Feel and Act?" 2016).

The four main energy characteristic colors are listed below with their meanings and how our bodies and minds react to them (Figure 4.1).

Cool blue: cautious, precise, deliberate, questioning, formal
Earth green: caring, encouraging, sharing, patient, relaxed
Sunshine yellow: sociable, dynamic, demonstrative, enthusiastic, persuasive
Fiery red: competitive, demanding, determined, strong-willed, purposeful

A wide range of theories from culture, science, and religion can help us understand how to use colors. In applying color to user interfaces, we must consider some of these aspects to match the use of color to the user interface (Meerwein, Rodeck, and Mahnke 2007).

4. Psychology of Color

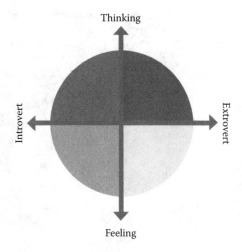

Thinking

Introvert

Extrovert

Feeling

Figure 4.1 **(See color insert.)**

Color energies diagram.

Visual Perception of the Brain

The relationships between visual perception and interfaces have evolved rapidly since early digital-computing interfaces, including the way in which we interact with them. The ergonomics of visual interaction in the past usually involved sitting at a desk. Now, however, we have interfaces almost everywhere, from cars to ATM machines. Our entire environment involves interfaces, one way or another, whether we are young or old.

Our brain required adjustment to all these changes. Not all screens are the same. In 1990, computer screens were very low in resolution compared with today because of computers' memory capacities. Our visual perception has adjusted accordingly.

Color System

Digital interfaces use the RGB color system, which stands for *red, green, and blue.* Zooming into any screen, you can see how RGB pixels are arranged to create colors. This process is called *additive color,* which is a very different method compared with using oils or any other type of physical paint. Physical colors are mixed to create subtractive color, which is based on red, yellow, and blue as primary. We use both types of color systems daily, from watching TV to reading a printed book. Figure 4.2 shows how the process of light creates the various colors we distinguish with our eyes.

The wonderful miracle of our visual system allows us to enjoy, interact, and experience the world around us. This system comprises two main parts: first, the brain, which does all the complex processing of imagery, and second, the eye, which

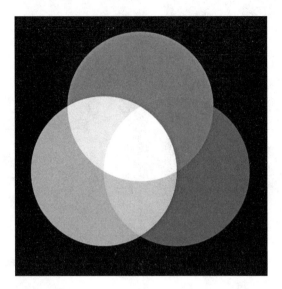

Figure 4.2 **(See color insert.)**

Red, green, and blue mixed on a screen, which always contains a black background. Mixing all three colors yields white.

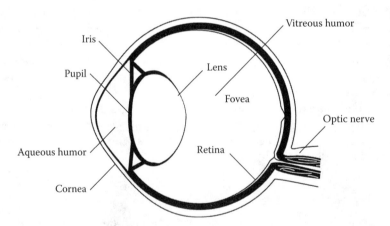

Figure 4.3

Diagram of the eye.

receives light rays in the visual wavelengths of the electromagnetic spectrum, usually 300–700 nm (Figure 4.3). The eye receives light and sends an electrical signal to the brain through the optic nerve. Light passes through the eye in the following order: cornea, aqueous humor, iris, lens, vitreous humor, and finally retina.

The cornea is a transparent layer. The iris creates a round aperture, varying in size. When bright light enters the eye, the iris gets smaller, while when it is dark, the iris dilates and expands. The fovea is the area where human vision is the sharpest. The retina recognizes light rays with photoreceptors, which send electrical signals. The eye has two types of photoreceptors, rods and cones. There are around 100 million rods in the human eye, located mostly evenly across the retina, with the exception of the fovea. There are only 6–7 million cones, which are located around the fovea, with some also found in the retina.

The human eye has three types of vision: (1) scotopic, which is night vision; (2) photopic, which is day vision; and (3) mesopic vision, which is in between, in light that is neither too dark nor too bright.

Three different types of cones help the human eye define color, one defining violet to blue and the other two cones defining cyan to red. The outcome of defining the colors the cones receive is called *trichromacy*.

Trichromacy not only helps the retina to perceive colors but also separates them, creating hierarchy and proportion in the foreground and background through the received light, resulting in the perception of contrast (Figure 4.4).

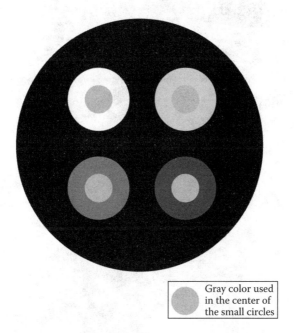

Gray color used in the center of the small circles

Figure 4.4

Contrast effect from lighter to darker backgrounds.

Gestalt Theory

The gestalt psychology movement was started by Max Wertheimer in the early 1900s. Gestalt theory is based on observing and analyzing our visual experience. For example, sometimes our visual perception could see an illusion or create an image or motion that was not meant to be there (see Figures 4.5 through 4.8).

Figure 4.5

Applying gestalt theory: the rounded circles with openings on one side and the luminosity in the space between create a white triangle.

Figure 4.6

Dalmatian in the middle. (Courtesy of Marr, D., et al., *Vision: A Computational Investigation into the Human Representation and Processing of Visual Information*, MIT Press, 2010.)

Figure 4.7

Image perceived as a rabbit or a duck. (Courtesy of Duck or Rabbit? The Image That Tells You How Creative You Are, 2016, *The Independent*, http://www.independent.co.uk/news/science/duck-or-rabbit-the-100-year-old-optical-illusion-that-tells-you-how-creative-you-are-a6873106.html.)

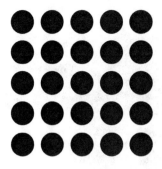

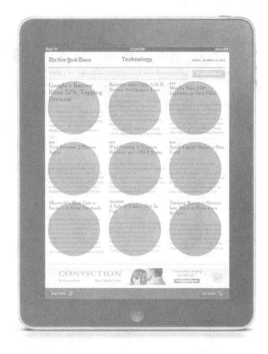

Figure 4.8

Sample source application: iPad release of the *New York Times* Editor's Choice. (Courtesy of Viticci, F., and Viticci, F., 2016, *The New York Times* Pulls Editor's Choice, Releases Free Full-Content App, https://www.macstories.net/ipad/the-new-york-times-pulls-editors-choice-releases-freefull-content-app/.)

This theory should always be applied to interfaces. By receiving feedback in testing, the UI designer will truly learn whether the interface is achieving its intended purpose. The laws of gestalt principles are: proximity, symmetry, closure, similarity, common fate, continuity, and figure/ground. The following examples will clarify their application.

1. *Proximity*: Are the objects grouped? What about the distance between objects? Does this affect our perception?

    Objects, including text, should have a well-balanced space to create a grouping of related items together.
2. *Symmetry*: This law reinforces alignment and constant relationships from object to object. In addition, symmetry means alignment across distances and even patterns, if objects are repeated (Figure 4.9).
3. *Closure*: This law refers to white space. Closure is usually considered to be a separate object, because it creates its own space (Figure 4.10).

Figure 4.9

Coleman, Symmetry Diagram using Kiss-Mix front page website. (Courtesy of Kiss Mix, 2016, http://www.kiss-mix.com/cocktails/.)

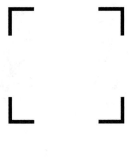
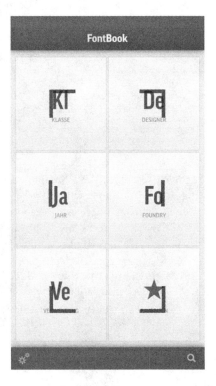

Figure 4.10

Sample website: Font Shop. (Courtesy of The World's Best Fonts for Print, Screen and Web, 2016, *FontShop*, https://www.fontshop.com/.)

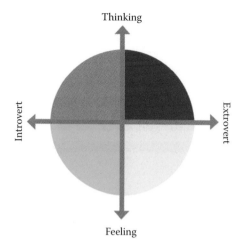

Figure 4.1

Color energies diagram.

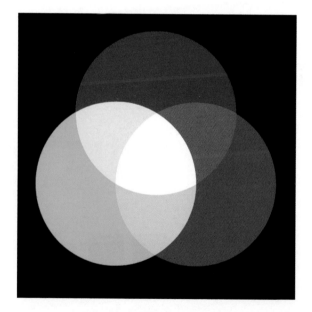

Figure 4.2

Red, green, and blue mixed on a screen, which always contains a black background. Mixing all three colors yields white.

Figure 4.15

Flag of the United States.

Figure 4.16

Colors bring emotion: diagram by CoSchedule. (Courtesy of CoSchedule, 2016, Color Psychology In Marketing: The Complete Guide [Free Download], *CoSchedule Blog*, http://coschedule.com/blog/color-psychology-marketing/.)

Figure 4.17

An RGB (red, green, and blue) image containing millions of colors.

Color wheel

Red • Green • Blue

Color mode: Additive

Primary colors = P

Secondary colors = S

Tertiary colors = T

Photoshop RGB color slider

Primary
Red
R = 255
G = 0
B = 0
P

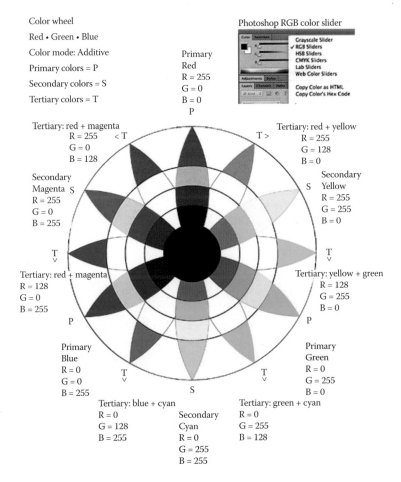

Tertiary: red + magenta
R = 255   < T
G = 0
B = 128

Secondary
Magenta S
R = 255
G = 0
B = 255

T
ᵛ

Tertiary: red + magenta
R = 128
G = 0
B = 255

P

Primary
Blue
R = 0
G = 0
B = 255

T
ᵛ

Tertiary: blue + cyan
R = 0
G = 128
B = 255

Secondary
Cyan
R = 0
G = 255
B = 255

Tertiary: red + yellow
T >   R = 255
G = 128
B = 0

Secondary
S Yellow
R = 255
G = 255
B = 0

T
ᵛ

Tertiary: yellow + green
R = 128
G = 255
B = 0

P

Primary
Green
R = 0
G = 255
B = 0

T
ᵛ

Tertiary: green + cyan
R = 0
G = 255
B = 128

S

Figure 4.18

Complex RGB color wheel including primary, secondary, and tertiary colors. (Courtesy of Carole, R.B., 2016, Digital Color Required Supplies, http://crbsite.com/new_aicasf/digital_color_current/dc_color_wheels.html.)

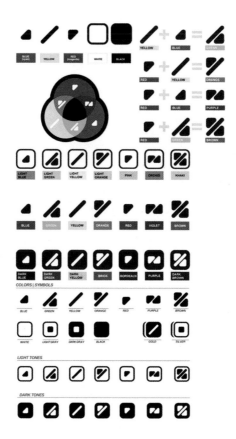

Figure 4.19

Basic color system using symbolism from ColorADD. (Courtesy of ColorADD, 2016, http://www.coloradd.net.)

Figure 4.21

World of Warcraft version 6.1 has a mode setting for colorblind users. (Courtesy of New Colorblind Support in Patch 6.1—WoW, 2016, *World of Warcraft*, http://worldofwarcraft.com/en-us/news/17964863.)

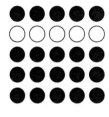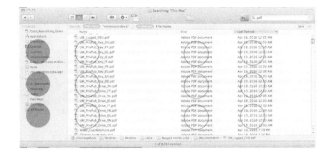

Figure 4.11

Apple OS window showing a list of PDF files.

4. *Similarity*: Objects should seem to be grouped intentionally (Figure 4.11).
5. *Common Fate*: Objects in motion within a group should have a similar motion, termed *common fate*. The motion might not even be very noticeable. In interfaces, for example, we have very subtle motions for links, slideshows, drop-down menus, and loaders (Figure 4.12).

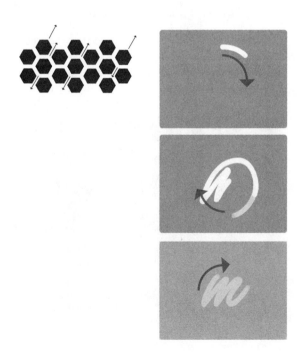

Figure 4.12

Animated logo in the Marvel app. (Courtesy of Free Mobile & Web Prototyping [iOS, Android] for Designers—Marvel, 2016, *Marvel Prototyping*, https://marvelapp.com/.)

6. *Continuity*: Forms should be continuous, and when sections are not filled we should note that our perception will fill them automatically (Figure 4.13).

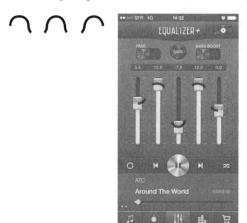

Figure 4.13

Equalizer app. (Courtesy of DJiT, 2016, Equalizer + : Free Music Player, Bass Booster and Sound Visualizer on the *App Store*. *App Store*, https://itunes.apple.com/us/app/equalizer-+-free-music-player/id777191669?mt=8.)

7. *Figure/Ground*: There should be a clear hierarchy between the interface's background and foreground. This law is extremely important concerning images, patterns, or colors placed in the background. The background should not be busy or distracting, allowing us to embrace the more important foreground (Figures 4.14 and 4.15).

Figure 4.14

Kindle app: book choices to read from your library of purchased items.

Figure 4.15 **(See color insert.)**

Flag of the United States.

Color as Emotion

Because color influences our emotions, it is important to understand the meaning of basic colors and have some idea of how the majority of users will receive the colors chosen for an interface. Color, by itself, is incredibly expressive. For example, consider the flag of the United States (Figure 4.10): anyone who lives in the United States can easily distinguish it, even from far away, because of its red and white stripes and stars on a blue field. Anyone who sees those colors and is familiar with the United States will immediately relate them to the US flag.

Our brains contain so much information, and whatever we receive we attempt to relate or make a connection to something that has happened or that we have seen in the past, especially if a color is associated with an emotion (Figure 4.16). People have favorite colors or hate certain colors, and so the relationship between a user and colors becomes very personal.

All the colors above have meaning, defining the general relationship between users and colors through emotion. However, there are always exceptions. Some users will have an external influence, whether from culture or a personal life experience, that will not exactly match with the diagram above (Figure 4.16). This is important to note, especially if the interface is geared toward social purposes.

Color Theory

To explain the wide range of definitions and studies of color would require several books. Here is a summarized version of the essentials for visual experiences in interfaces. As mentioned earlier, computer interfaces use RGB colors (Figure 4.17), identified by a numerical value. For example, black is 0,0,0, which may also be expressed in hexadecimal numbers (HEX). Each value of red, green, and blue ranges, in decimal, from 0 to 255 (0,0,0 is black and 255,255,255 is white). It is easy for an interface developer to apply colors chosen in RGB and HEX values. Using CMYK—cyan, magenta, yellow, key (black)—colors is not recommended, because that system should only be used for printed color.

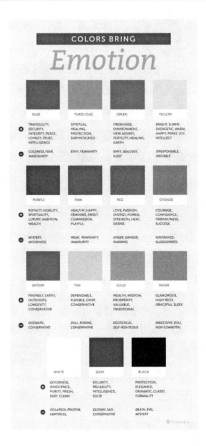

Figure 4.16 **(See color insert.)**

Colors bring emotion: diagram by CoSchedule. (Courtesy of CoSchedule, 2016, Color Psychology In Marketing: The Complete Guide [Free Download], *CoSchedule Blog*, http://coschedule.com/blog/color-psychology-marketing/.)

Figure 4.17 **(See color insert.)**

An RGB (red, green, and blue) image containing millions of colors.

4. Psychology of Color

The first step to choosing colors is to choose the basic, secondary, or even the tertiary colors (Figure 4.18). Once you have chosen one of them, you can go more in depth if you are looking, for example, for a softer or lighter version.

Primary colors: Red, blue, and yellow.

Secondary colors: Orange, purple, and green. Created by mixing the primary colors together.

Tertiary colors: Six shades made from mixing primary and secondary colors.

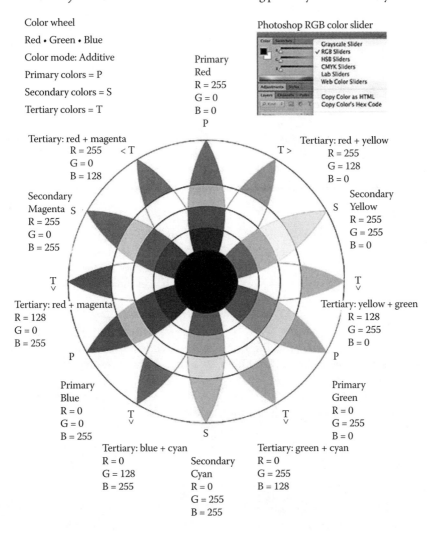

Color wheel

Red • Green • Blue

Color mode: Additive

Primary colors = P

Secondary colors = S

Tertiary colors = T

Photoshop RGB color slider

Grayscale Slider
✓ RGB Sliders
HSB Sliders
CMYK Sliders
Lab Sliders
Web Color Sliders

Copy Color as HTML
Copy Color's Hex Code

Primary
Red
R = 255
G = 0
B = 0
P

Tertiary: red + magenta
R = 255
G = 0
B = 128
< T

T >
Tertiary: red + yellow
R = 255
G = 128
B = 0

Secondary
Magenta S
R = 255
G = 0
B = 255

S Secondary
Yellow
R = 255
G = 255
B = 0

Tertiary: red + magenta
R = 128
G = 0
B = 255

Tertiary: yellow + green
R = 128
G = 255
B = 0

Primary
Blue
R = 0
G = 0
B = 255

Primary
Green
R = 0
G = 255
B = 0

Tertiary: blue + cyan
R = 0
G = 128
B = 255

Secondary
Cyan
R = 0
G = 255
B = 255

Tertiary: green + cyan
R = 0
G = 255
B = 128

Figure 4.18 **(See color insert.)**

Complex RGB color wheel including primary, secondary, and tertiary colors. (Courtesy of Carole, R.B., 2016, Digital Color Required Supplies, http://crbsite.com/new_aicasf/digital_color_current/dc_color_wheels.html.)

There are various ways to classify color, but the most helpful are as follows: (1) *tint*, lightening a color by adding more white; (2) *shade*, darkening a color by adding more black; and (3) *tone*, which is a way of darkening by adding gray.

When choosing a color or colors, the first step is to list options and to explore in depth how a user will feel emotionally and mentally about that color. Remember, an interface is a visual experience; we are immersed in the application or website. After choosing your first option or options, it might be necessary to choose a complementary color, which is usually the opposite color on the color wheel. For example, for blue, the complementary color is yellow. When choosing complementary colors, it is extremely important to remain aware of color-blindness restrictions. More information about color blindness is presented later in this chapter.

Analogous Colors

You usually choose two primary colors, with a third, secondary color that is a combination of the two. Make sure to make the colors proportional, using the rule of 60%, 30%, 10%. Pick a dominant color (60%), and use the other ones perhaps in links or in menus, or anywhere else to highlight (30% and 10%). Find a balance: not too noisy and not too quiet. For example, if you decided on blue and red as a second, the third will be purple.

Triadic Colors

When adding a third color into the mix, the interface must be balanced, with none of the colors overwhelming the experience. For children it is a different case, because children love lively color, and so you can arrange colors more flexibly and spontaneously. Even in such circumstances, however, it is important to balance the atmosphere in the use of color.

Tetradic Colors

The more colors added into the mix, the more complex and more difficult it becomes to arrange them. Sometimes, it is extremely necessary to add color because of the importance of information. Avoid using too many colors, however, as it will be overwhelming not only for you as the designer but also for the user. Find a balance and use similarities. For example, if choosing red and orange, then probably the other two colors will use the same tint or shade or be completely opposite (light blue and dark blue). Make sure to balance opposite colors in the interface.

Color Blindness

According to statistics, one out of every 12 men and one out of every 200 women are colorblind, so over 2.7 million people worldwide are colorblind (Color Blindness Awareness, 2017). Therefore, it is extremely important to consider this matter as a priority in interface design. Several helpful tools have been created to help colorblind people translate the meanings of color through symbolism. The example below, called *Color ADD*, is an entire system to help colorblind individuals (Figure 4.19).

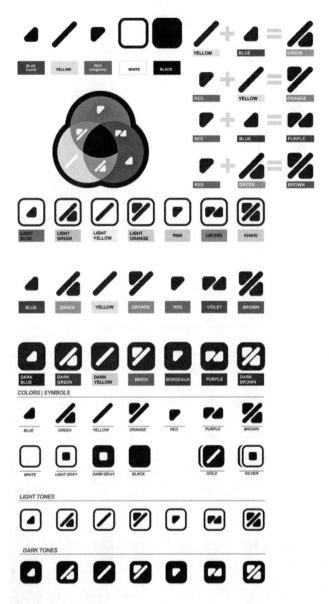

Figure 4.19 **(See color insert.)**

Basic color system using symbolism from ColorADD. (Courtesy of ColorADD, 2016, http://www.coloradd.net.)

There are many types of color blindness, some mild and some severe. When someone has color blindness, the eye does not register some hues. Color blindness may be classified as follows: (1) *protanopia* means loss of vision of the red hue, known as *L cones*; (2) *deuteranopia* means loss of red, orange, and yellow vision;

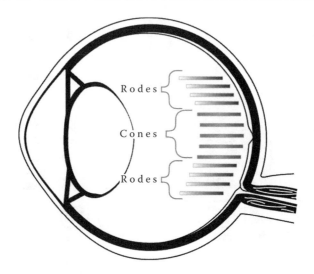

Figure 4.20

Diagram of the eye, showing cones and rods, which are essential for humans to perceive all colors.

(3) *tritanopia* means loss of indigo, blue, and violet vision; and (4) *monochromacy*, which usually means everything the person sees is blue, known as *S cone*. On some rare occasions, people only see everything in green, which is known as the *M cone*, or in red (L cone), which is the rarest type (Figure 4.20).

It is important to add some type of vision mode (Figure 4.21) or colorblind settings (Figure 4.22) into an interface. It need not incorporate all the options above, unless it is an app or website geared solely to colorblind users.

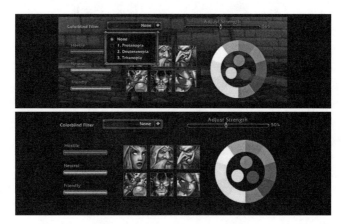

Figure 4.21 **(See color insert.)**

World of Warcraft version 6.1 has a mode setting for colorblind users. (Courtesy of New Colorblind Support in Patch 6.1—WoW, 2016, *World of Warcraft*, http://worldofwarcraft.com/en-us/news/17964863.)

4. Psychology of Color

Figure 4.22

Online tool to help learn more about color blindness and visual solutions. (Courtesy of Colblindor | All about Color Blindness, 2016, http://www.colorblindness.com.)

Ten Commandments of Color Interaction

Aaron Marcus has written ten commandments of color interaction. His guidance concerns not only color but also type readability and usability. It is extremely important to work very closely with color, type, and image, because these are the ingredients of a successful user interface layout. In the article ("Color My UX Readable | ACM Interactions" 2016) from IX Interactions, Aaron Marcus gives the ten commandments as follows:

1. Use a maximum of five, plus or minus two, colors.
2. Use foveal (center) and peripheral colors appropriately.
3. Use colors that exhibit a minimum shift in color/size if the colors change in size in the imagery.
4. Do not use high chroma, or spectrally extreme colors, simultaneously.
5. Use familiar, consistent color codings, with appropriate references.
6. Use the same color for grouping related elements.
7. Use the same color code for applications, training, testing, and publications.
8. Use high value and high saturation colors to draw attention.
9. If possible, use redundant coding of shape as well as color.
10. Use color to enhance black-and-white information.

References

Birren, Faber. 1984. *Color & Human Response: Aspects of Light and Color Bearing on the Reactions of Living Things and the Welfare of Human Beings*. Wiley, New York.

Birren, Faber. 2013. *Color Psychology and Color Therapy: A Factual Study of the Influence of Color on Human Life*. Martino Fine Books, Whitefish, MT.

Can Color Really Change How You Feel and Act? 2016. *Verywell.* Accessed July 31, 2016. https://www.verywell.com/color-psychology-2795824.

Colblindor | All about Color Blindness. 2016. Accessed July 31, 2016. http://www.color-blindness.com.

ColorADD. 2016. Accessed July 31, 2016. http://www.coloradd.net.

Color Blindness Awareness. 2017. Accessed June 13, 2017. http://www.colour-blindawareness.org/colour-blindness/.

ACM Interactions. Color My UX Readable. 2016. Accessed July 31, 2016. http://interactions.acm.org/blog/view/color-my-ux-readable.

CoSchedule. 2016. Color Psychology In Marketing: The Complete Guide [Free Download]. *CoSchedule Blog.* Accessed April 21, 2017. http://coschedule.com/blog/color-psychology-marketing/.

Carole. R. Brown. 2016. Digital Color Required Supplies. Accessed July 31, 2016. http://crbsite.com/new_aicasf/digital_color_current/dc_color_wheels.html.

DJiT. 2016. Equalizer + : Free Music Player, Bass Booster and Sound Visualizer on the App Store. *App Store.* Accessed July 31, 2016. https://itunes.apple.com/us/app/equalizer-+-free-music-player/id777191669?mt=8.

Duck or Rabbit? The Image That Tells You How Creative You Are. 2016. *The Independent.* Accessed April 21, 2017. http://www.independent.co.uk/news/science/duck-or-rabbit-the-100-year-old-optical-illusion-that-tells-you-how-creative-you-are-a6873106.html.

Free Mobile & Web Prototyping (iOS, Android) for Designers—Marvel. 2016. *Marvel Prototyping.* Accessed July 31, 2016. https://marvelapp.com/.

Gage, John. 1999a. *Color and Culture: Practice and Meaning from Antiquity to Abstraction.* University of California Press, Oakland, CA.

Gage, John. 1999b. *Color and Meaning: Art, Science, and Symbolism.* University of California Press, Oakland, CA.

Kiss Mix. 2016. Website. Accessed July 31, 2016. http://www.kiss-mix.com/cocktails/.

Marr, David, ShimonUllman, and Tomaso A.Poggio. 2010. *Vision: A Computational Investigation into the Human Representation and Processing of Visual Information.* MIT Press, Cambridge, MA.

Meerwein, Gerhard, BettinaRodeck, and Frank H.Mahnke. 2007. *Color—Communication in Architectural Space.* Walter de Gruyter, Berlin, Germany.

New Colorblind Support in Patch 6.1—WoW. 2016. *World of Warcraft.* Accessed July 31, 2016. http://worldofwarcraft.com/en-us/news/17964863.

Viticci, Federico, and Federico Viticci. 2016. *The New York Times* Pulls Editor's Choice, Releases Free Full-Content App. Accessed July 31, 2016. https://www.macstories.net/ipad/the-new-york-times-pulls-editors-choice-releases-free-full-content-app/.

The World's Best Fonts for Print, Screen and Web. 2016. *FontShop.* Accessed July 31, 2016. https://www.fontshop.com/.

5

Typography, Icons, and User Legibility

Introduction to Typography for Interfaces

Initial user interfaces (UIs) for computers, such as the Xerox Alto, were solely typographic and thus did not include icons. Therefore, historically typography was a significant part of the visual origins of computing, from coding to the visual interface. Along with software and technology, the graphical user interface (GUI) has developed rapidly over several decades, and its increased resolution has provided visual designers with more flexibility, removing limitations. Early computer screens were black and white, and so the introduction of color resulted in many new opportunities for software development and GUI design. For further information about the history of GUIs, please revisit Chapter 1, which discusses the subject in detail.

The majority of users know and recognize interface typography in desktop computers, but over time GUIs have spread to various devices for different purposes, including cars, phones, wearables, interactive ads, and interactive directories. Typography is a necessary element of an interface and thus not something designers choose to add; whether it is a word in an interactive ad or an entire typographic system in an app, interface typography is everywhere. Research suggests that 95% ("Web Design Is 95% Typography | iA" 2016) of web interface content is fully typographic, and thus typography is considered to be the lifeblood of interfaces, without which users can neither understand nor interact with the interface.

Brief Highlights of the History of Typefaces for Interfaces

Interface typefaces emerged abruptly because of the limitations of the screens, which were small in size and lacked color. Typeface characters are created and compacted into a typeface through an embedding process, enabling each character to be saved as an image. Typeface-creation software packs all the letterforms to create a typeface after the typographer spaces and aligns the characters. Therefore, exploring the way typography is arranged and structured in interfaces, all letters or characters are single images embedded in the interface. This is a very important concept, because layouts require simplicity and typographic hierarchy, with the latter often including more typeface weights that can include specifics such as regular, italic, and bold. Interfaces can have size limitations depending on their intended device. For example, an Android app is limited to 1 MB of memory, which must be considered when designing an interface for this platform. Not only do designers have to create a successful typographic design, but they also must follow these rules and limitations. When it comes to interfaces for websites, a 1 MB limit must also be observed in the home page size, although an even lower page size of 500 KB is recommended, because download speeds vary from country to country. If the website is to have global appeal, it is necessary to keep in mind these various limitations. In addition, typographic weights and their limitations will affect the load and the speed optimization of any interface. It is vital that interface designers know the human standards guidelines of the device for which they are designing, because this will help ensure that the interface succeeds. Overall, though the limitations mentioned above might change over time due to improvements in computing memory capacity, it will always be important for the visual designer to bear in mind that pages, windows, menus, and content should be simple, effective, and to the point; information overload should be avoided.

Typographic Format Timeline

1968

In 1968, the first digital typeface was created for typesetting, book publishing, and other general purposes (Figure 5.1). This sans serif typeface was widely used because it pioneered digital cathode ray tube phototypesetting.

1973

Five years later, the Xerox Alto Mono font was created and used in the first GUI (Figures 5.2 and 5.3). However, this GUI was not designed to be a part of the

Figure 5.1

Typeface Digi Grotesk S was the first digital typeface, designed by Dr. Ing. Rudolf Hell. (Courtesy of This Was The First Computer Font, 2016, *Pinterest,* https://www. pinterest.com/pin/238831586459213533/.)

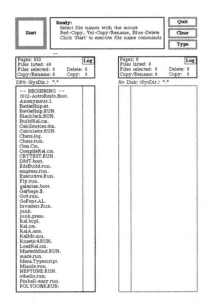

Figure 5.2

The Xerox Alto computer, released in the 1970s, had the first GUI. Its typography did not have a clear hierarchy, with only two weights, nor did the layout provide the user with a strong sense of hierarchy.

marketplace; instead it was a research project of the lab. This bitmap typeface worked well at the screen resolutions of the time.

1983

Susan Kare designed Chicago, a bitmapped, sans serif typeface, for the first Apple Macintosh, which proved to be a drastic change for Apple computers (Figure 5.4). Up to that point, they lacked a branded typeface that defined them as Apple.

Figure 5.3

Xerox Alto Mono was the typeface used in the first graphical interface for computers. (Courtesy of Damieng, 2016, https://images.damieng.com/fonts/converted/AltoMono.png.)

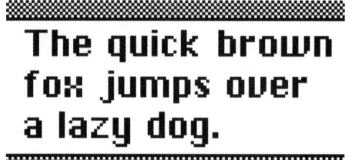

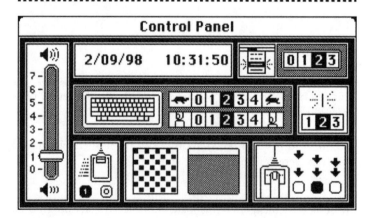

Figure 5.4

The typeface Chicago was designed solely for Apple computers.

5. Typography, Icons, and User Legibility

Bitmap

A bitmap is the entire visual interface, including images and typography. The word *bitmap* derives from computer programming terminology: "a map of bits." Bitmaps cannot be scaled or maintain small resolution because of the way they are created. In addition, a bitmap has two colors, which can include black and white (Figure 5.5). The advantage of these bitmap fonts is that they can be edited by type designers, unlike the previous method, photosetting. Because of the low resolution available at the beginning of interfaces for computers, such fonts were carefully edited pixel by pixel, which enhanced readability during that period. To learn more about pixels and resolution, please see Chapter 6. The disadvantage of this format is that each typeface weight had to be a font on its own. Therefore, fonts took up a lot of space in software.

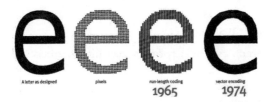

Figure 5.5

Types of letterforms displayed in screen interfaces. (Courtesy of Designhistory, 2016, Early Technologies of Digital Type, http://www.designhistory.org/Digital_Revolution_pages/EarlyDigType.html.)

Outlined Fonts

Outline fonts, also known as *vectors*, appeared in 1974. They use Bézier curves and mathematical formulas to create each letter form, also known as *glyphs*, which allows the letters to be scaled to any size. This type of font was groundbreaking at the time, and because of its accessibility it influenced the creation of the language PostScript, which was later created by Adobe between 1982 and 1984. This helped not only typefaces but also all types of graphics, many of which we still use to this day.

True Type

True Type was created in the late 1980s and became a standard, remaining so to this day. This font file standard was created by Microsoft and Apple, and the rendering method helped improve the resolution of typography on the screens of that time. The first typefaces converted to this font type were Times New Roman, Helvetica, Courier, and Pi. In addition, Apple replaced some of their fonts in their operating system.

Font Hinting

As a method to refine and make fonts more legible, font hinting can be used on certain types of screens ("Typotheque: Font Hinting by Peter Biľak" 2016).

Open Type

Created by Microsoft between 1994 and 1997, with Apple joining in the effort in 1996, Open Type is a collaborative effort between the two companies and is thus cross-platform.

Embedded Open Type

Created by Microsoft, embedded open type (EOT) supports all Internet Explorer browsers.

Web Open Font Format

The web open font format (WOFF, WOFF2) was created solely for web font interfaces.

Scalable Vector Graphics

Scalable vector graphics (SVG) is the largest file type because of the way it is compressed, and, as such, it is better used in interfaces for icons and custom graphics.

Fonts for OTF extension files in apps can be used on most platforms, although Android platforms prefer TTF. It is important to ensure that you follow the guidelines and use the correct extensions of the OS on which you are building your app.

Web Typography

The history of web fonts started with Tim Berners Lee, who created the first World Wide Web page on December 12, 1990, although it only used the default font at that time, which was Times New Roman. Over time, typefaces were added, setting a standard of at least 14 typefaces (six serif, six sans serif, and two monospaced). Initially, typefaces were not designed specifically for the web, primarily because designers were still preoccupied with designing and shaping them for print, but due to the need to have such web-friendly typefaces, those such as Times New Roman became part of the default options. Designers initially wanted to use certain typefaces but, in order to do so, had to save them as flat images just to be able to place them on the web. These images were not searchable, and the only interactive option was to make them a hotspot for linking somewhere. This design slowed down the loading of pages and sometimes frustrated users. In the mid-1990s, a typographer named Matthew Carter was tasked with the design of screen fonts, and the resulting styles, Georgia and Verdana, have become widely used. In addition, Carter designed Tahoma for Windows. Since then, things have changed, and now we enjoy the option of placing custom fonts on websites through various providers.

Figure 5.6

Font anatomy.

Figure 5.7

Serif vs. sans serif and stress.

X-Height

As the center, the x-height is where all typefaces are located, beginning where each one sits and is aligned, and at the top they do the same. The only exception is old-style characters, which go over and below the x-height. Overall, the x-height is a very important part of legibility, because it holds the central structure of all letterforms.

In order for these forms to be legible and reader-friendly, they need to have large openings in all letter forms, such as in *a* or *e*. Everything should be open, including the length of the descender and ascender. Overall, letterforms should maintain constant balance. The reason why letters need taller x-heights is because this makes the text more readable. Most interfaces are accessed while in motion, including wearable interfaces like watches and other non-portable ones such as desktops, vending machines, or ATMs. But regardless of the interface, humans today feel pressured to get everything done as fast as possible. We want food in less than a minute and access to everything in seconds, including access to interfaces. Users do not want to spend a lot of time trying to read. For example, if a user accesses a website but cannot read the information in less than 10 seconds, they are likely to go somewhere else. Therefore, it is more than essential to choose a typeface that can deliver users the best readability. In addition, if there is too much information in an app and if the letterforms are not large enough for the reader, the user will likely delete the app in seconds.

Line Height

Understanding the purpose of the x-height is essential for determining the line height, because the distance between baselines determines the line height. This value will vary according to the shape and form of the typeface, as well as according to the texture formed by the paragraph.

Letter Spacing

Letter spacing is essential, since without it, individual letters can become crowded in a word, sentence, and then paragraph. It is vital that text not be left to default letter spacing, because just a slight alteration by only a few pixels will make a huge difference. It is essential to spend time type-spacing letterforms.

General Tips When Setting Your Type

When setting your type, it is essential to analyze the letterforms individually, before doing the same with words, sentences, paragraphs, and even columns. Everything starts with getting to know the details of the letterforms, including whether one is a serif or sans serif font, analyzing stress, considering the thickness of the strokes, and much more. It is a good idea to enlarge the typeface as much as possible in order to see it better. Once you are familiar with the letterforms, it will be easier to use the texture that together produces the sentences and even columns. In addition, this will drastically help navigation, because by now you will know under which circumstances it would be best to use small caps, lower case, or upper and lower case. The paragraph texture determines readability.

Columns

When working in columns, it is best to work first with the smallest screen size for the interface; then, if you are creating a responsive app or website, it will be easy to adjust the layout.

Most likely, you will only fit about 95% in one column, which is usually four to seven words per line for a mobile device such as a smartphone. If such a device's interface has a desktop version, it is recommended you add more columns, because the first layout created will look forced when on a desktop if not designed proportionally to a larger size (Figure 5.8). For wearables, the text is severely restricted because of the size. Text cannot go beyond reading text messages or any small piece of information such as headlines or summaries. Usually, the text on each line does not have more than three to five words at a time if a column is used on this type of device.

Figure 5.8

News360 app for mobile devices, including the wearable Apple Watch. This app updates the user with news throughout the day. (Courtesy of News 360 Inc, https://itunes.apple.com/us/app/news360-your-personalized-news-reader/id420397564?mt=8.)

There are approximately 12–17 basic typefaces that are standards for interfaces used in the majority of operating systems (for both web and apps):

> *Sans typeface*: Helvetica, Verdana, Arial, Trebuchet MS, Android Sans
> *Sans typeface mono*: Roboto, Android Sans Mono
> *Serif typeface*: Calibri, Candara, Corbel, Times New Roman
> *Slab serif*: Courier New

Other types of interfaces that are more customized for specific devices (e.g., an ATM or TV) will not fit to these standard typefaces (Figure 5.9). In all those cases, it is suggested that the designer considers the operating system that is being used and then download all of these free fonts and add them to the interface by installing them on the device. This rule remains valid when purchasing custom fonts.

Great custom font stores:

1. FontShop at http://fontshop.com
2. Typotheque at http://typotheque.com
3. Monotype at http://fonts.com
4. Hoefler & Co. at http://typography.com
5. Adobe Typekit at http://typekit.com (mostly web interfaces at this time)
6. Letters from Sweden at http://lettersfromsweden.se/custom/
7. Google Fonts at http://www.google.com/fonts
8. Process Type Foundry at http://processtypefoundry.com/

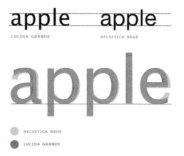

apple apple
LUCIDA GRANDE   HELVETICA NEUE

apple

HELVETICA NEUE
LUCIDA GRANDE

Figure 5.9

Comparison of x-height between Lucida Grande and Helvetica Neue. In 2014, the Apple OS stopped using the former and switched to the latter. (Courtesy of Covert, A., 2014, Why Apple's New Font Won't Work On Your Desktop, *Co. Design*, http://www.fastcodesign.com/3031432/why-apples-newfont-wont-work-on-your-desktop.)

New Era for Replacing Fonts (Figures 5.10 through 5.14)

Sartorially significant and glittering with bullion braid and gold lace

ARRIVING 1936

FLORAL SPACING ADJUSTMENT CONSIDERED COMPLETE

Blue Fibers

Circles fashioned of wool and cotton twill became standard

Figure 5.10

Elena. (Courtesy of Process Type Foundry, 2016, Elena Font Family, http://processtypefoundry.com/fonts/elena/.)

Prüfungsanweisungen

Újságcím

Stichwort

Bezeichnung

Figure 5.11

Typeface fedra mono screen. (Courtesy of Typotheque: Fedra Mono Screen Font Family, 2016, https://www.typotheque.com/fonts/fedra_mono_screen.)

Vita Medium 200px

Titulek

Vita Medium

It seems to be a golden age of type design—not only
are there more type foundries now than ever before,
not only is distribution easier and more direct, not
only is type a hot topic for numerous specialised
blogs and magazines, but even the general interest
media are in on the conversation, (if only
occasionally). New type design courses are opening
regularly, churning out legions of type designers. And
there are now over 150,000 fonts available for direct
download.

Vita Medium 16px

Figure 5.12

Typeface Vita. (Courtesy of Typotheque: Vita Font Family, 2016, https://www.
typotheque.com/fonts/vita.)

Forza ScreenSmart Light. Its squared
Forza ScreenSmart Light

Forza ScreenSmart Light Italic. Its ital
Forza ScreenSmart Light Italic

Forza ScreenSmart Book. Simultaneo
Forza ScreenSmart Book

Forza ScreenSmart Book Italic. Living
Forza ScreenSmart Book Italic

Forza ScreenSmart Medium. Redesig
Forza ScreenSmart Medium

Forza ScreenSmart Medium Italic. Cla
Forza ScreenSmart Medium Italic

Forza ScreenSmart Bold. Throughou
Forza ScreenSmart Bold

Forza ScreenSmart Bold Italic. Geom
Forza ScreenSmart Bold Italic

Forza ScreenSmart Black. A font u
Forza ScreenSmart Black

Forza ScreenSmart Black Italic. Its
Forza ScreenSmart Black Italic

Figure 5.13

Typeface Forza. (Courtesy of Hoefler & Co., 2016.)

Whitney ScreenSmart Light. A new te
Whitney ScreenSmart Light

Whitney ScreenSmart Light Italic. An c
Whitney ScreenSmart Light Italic

Whitney ScreenSmart Book. A new w
Whitney ScreenSmart Book

Whitney ScreenSmart Book Italic. A w
Whitney ScreenSmart Book Italic

Whitney ScreenSmart Medium. Oper
Whitney ScreenSmart Medium

Whitney ScreenSmart Medium Italic.
Whitney ScreenSmart Medium Italic

Whitney ScreenSmart Semibold. A c
Whitney ScreenSmart Semibold

Whitney ScreenSmart Semibold Itali
Whitney ScreenSmart Semibold Italic

Whitney ScreenSmart Bold. Welcon
Whitney ScreenSmart Bold

Whitney ScreenSmart Bold Italic. Re
Whitney ScreenSmart Bold Italic

Figure 5.14

Typeface Whitney. (Courtesy of Whitney Fonts, 2016.)

Combining Typefaces

When choosing more than one typeface, the designer must have a very good reason for doing so, probably because of the need for more hierarchy in the content. When a designer uses two typefaces in a UI, it is usually because there is a lot of information and thus a need for higher division within the content so that the user can access it easily. If you have never experimented with combining typefaces, it is best to choose a sans serif and a serif typeface (Hoefler & Co 2016). Use your design intuition to decide which two you should work with. Obviously, it is often fine to add more typefaces, combining three or four, but be aware that it becomes more difficult to manage them, not only in the layout but also in terms of limitations of the app's capacity and even the loading time required for websites. Though the interface should be typographically beautiful, the loading should also be effective; establishing a balance between the two is crucial.

Font Files Workflow and Tools to Manage Fonts

As mentioned earlier in this chapter, various types of font file extensions will work well for the web, as well as for apps and software outside of the web. Do not use fonts that are specially geared toward printing purposes, because their resolutions and sizes are larger compared with fonts that are geared solely to the screen. Although these environments can sometimes work together, at other times they are not complementary. Therefore, it is necessary to know, for example, that for Android apps it is best to use TTF rather than OTF files, whereas the latter is more appropriate when designing Apple apps. Again, it is always best to consult with developers to learn more about what is compatible before purchasing a font.

Moreover, when using typography on the web, it is very important to know that four types of extensions are compatible with different browsers: TTF, EOT, WOFF/WOFF2, and SVG. The reason these different extensions exist is to make sure that every browser is able to accept a custom font.

Various software companies and foundries have created their own ways of providing custom fonts to the public, with some permitting their fonts to be used through a web server, others renting the typeface, and some allowing the fonts to be downloaded for unlimited or limited use. Make sure that you provide all this information to your client and add it to the budget at the beginning of the project.

Icons

Introduction to Semiotics

Semiotics is the study of signs and symbols and how they are used, including their meanings and interpretation. The discipline began with Charles Sanders Peirce (1839–1914), who created a classification of three main categories: icon, symbol, and index. Later, he established three branches of semiotics: syntax, semantics, and pragmatics. Syntax is the relationship between signs, whereas semantics refers to the relationship between the meaning of the sign and the graphic sign itself. Pragmatics is the relationship between the user and the sign.

Icon: Represents something pictorial that gives us a clear message. For example, the folder icon is generally used for software and organization (Figure 5.15).

Figure 5.15

Folder icon from the operating system Yosemite from Apple.

Index: Direct signs that do not generalize any of the information we are given. For example, a warning window in your operating system (Figure 5.16).

Figure 5.16

Window pop-up with a white exclamation point in a yellow triangle, serving to warn the user directly that something is wrong. (Courtesy of Support Apple, 2016, https://support.apple.com/en-us/HT200553.)

Symbol: Usually, this type of graphic has no logical relationship to the image (Figure 5.17), but everyone who knows about the image understands it automatically. For example, consider the sandwich symbol in our navigation bars (Figure 5.17). After using it, users become familiar with it.

Figure 5.17

Hamburger icon, which was created by Norm Cox for Xerox Star for the first GUI. This icon is ubiquitous nowadays, used to show where the navigation is located, and usually appears when we need to access a menu.

Visual Metaphors

Visual metaphors are representations of any type of object, person, place, or even an idea that becomes an image and should be easily understood by the user. When creating interfaces, whether small or large, it is vital to include visual metaphors, because we are unable to use only typography to describe all the functions of an interface. For example, a desktop for a computer requires a wide variety of metaphors, including the trash can metaphor and the clock. Everything that is not typographically written should have a graphical metaphor that is extremely easy to understand (Figure 5.18).

In addition, all visual metaphors should have some type of visual consistency, whether they have the same size, same outlines, or same stroke width. Overall, visual metaphors not only need to match in proportion but also relate as metaphors. For example, given a desktop metaphor for an operating system interface, you cannot start adding animals as visual metaphors, because you are not creating a farm; you are creating a desktop.

Figure 5.18

Trash, folder, and calculator metaphors. (Courtesy of Abhishek Bagul, 2015, http://1. bp.blogspot.com/-X-xXobZfKbl/UwGUeQVP77I/AAAAAAAAAAH0/x4ii7jssXKo/s1600/ The-Evolution-Of-Icon-Design.jpg.)

Icon Design

Introduction

Icon design is a small part of information design that has become more important than ever in the era of the Internet and computing, as we are all interconnected through social and other media. The world has become a global village. Because UIs are accessed globally, some parts of the UI need to use icons that ensure global applicability and fast access. When they are "tools," icons are usually used to cut, paste, zoom in, zoom out, play, and stop. All of these types of icons have become universal, and as such, regardless of their language, users are able to recognize them. Users subconsciously use icons as a result of their familiarity. It is important to keep all universal icons the same, because if we change the play icon to be similar to the stop icon, for example, it becomes ambiguous and confusing for the user, akin to attempting to change the letter *A* into the letter *D*. Therefore, following the universal icon language makes it easier for the UI designer and typographer to design icons.

A Brief History of Icons

The history of icons started when Otto Neurath (1882–1945) created the International System of Typographic Picture Education (Isotype) based on the theory that "words divide, pictures unite." Neurath was an economist, social scientist, and philosopher from Vienna, and, from childhood, he was fascinated by hieroglyphs. He became the head of the Housing Museum in Vienna and later initiated the Social and Economic Museum of Vienna, where his love for symbol-based language was displayed through museum exhibits on social information, and where he led a team of 25 people. He later married Marie Reidemeister, a mathematician and physicist who also attended art school. Isotype was a groundbreaking method of design, because it not only used imagery to represent words but also informed the audience through charts and maps and was capable of explaining complex ideas through graphics without words (Figure 5.19). At this moment the largest collection of Isotype is located at the University of Reading, known as the Otto and Marie Neurath Isotype Collection.

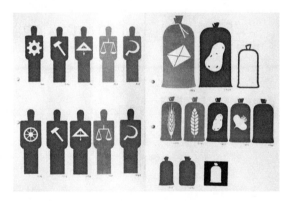

Figure 5.19

Isotype "picture dictionary." Leaf from binder, Gerd Arntz, 1929–1933, 300 × 225 mm. (Courtesy of I.C. 4/2.)

The Isotype picture dictionary was a working reference file of all pictograms designed by Gerd Arntz. It shows the grammatical aspects of isotype pictogram design, in which a symbol can be qualified or made into a kind of compound noun by combination with another. The symbols within the human figures here indicate different professions (Figure 5.20).

The same system is applied on the page to the right, where the contents of the sacks are represented by an image.

Some objects resist typification. For example, it seems almost impossible to design an immediately recognizable pictogram for "potato." Arntz's attempts are shown here in two different versions inside the middle sacks of the first two rows (CB).

From 1943 until his death in December 1945, Otto Neurath worked tirelessly on numerous versions of an innovative "visual autobiography" entitled *From Hieroglyphics to Isotype*. He initially conceived it as a picture book, "with a few

Figure 5.20

Cover design of *Tips for Tots*, a handcrafted mock-up made by the Neuraths as part of a proposal for a series of children's books, published by Max Parrish in 1944. By "Isotype world," the Neuraths meant an Isotype vocabulary, or consistent symbolic forms for people, animals, and houses, and a restricted color scheme and particular way of organizing these elements (SW). (Courtesy of Isotype Revisited.)

Figure 5.21

Cover design/mock-up of Otto Neurath's *From Hieroglyphics to Isotype* (Isotype Institute, c.1944, I.C. 3.2/87). (Courtesy of Isotype Revisited.)

explanatory notes only," adding that its purpose would be to "show the different sources from which Isotype has evolved." He wanted to reveal Isotype's genealogy by tracing it to its roots, looking at heraldic and allegorical imagery, tattoos and playing card symbols, military drawings and battle plans, maps, still and moving photographic images, and projection and perspective presentations (Figure 5.21). By doing so, it was possible to consider instances of how "the visual elements of a comprehensive visual language combine."

This historical overview gives us a guide to continue in the Neuraths' footsteps, by designing for the screen or for other surfaces regardless of their size.

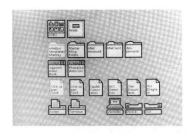

Figure 5.22

First icons of Xerox user interface computer.

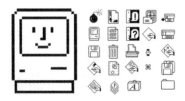

Figure 5.23

Susan Kare's icons from the first GUI of Apple Lisa. (Courtesy of Susan Kare Graphic Design, http://kare.com/apple-icons/.)

As UI designers, in addition to creating interfaces it is also our responsibility to educate and inform users, since our job is to make information as accessible as possible.

The first icons were created for Xerox in the 1970s and were mostly text inside icon folders. At this time, there were no UI designers. By the early 1980s, only a few such individuals had been hired, because companies did not see the value of visual design in UIs. Icons had to be extremely small and simple because computer memory was very limited, around 1 MB at maximum capacity. Therefore, icons were few and far between, which is why they used a lot of text, as illustrated in Figure 5.22.

Right after Xerox in 1984, the Apple Macintosh was released, with its groundbreaking UI. Susan Kare, one of the first recognized UI designers, was one of the people in charge of the Mac's icons, which were limited to a 30 × 30 pixel grid with a total of 900 pixels (Figure 5.23). According to Kare, every pixel was extremely important in every icon.

Workbench was the first UI to use four screen colors, but they were so strong as a result of the blue background that they caused eye strain and pain (Figure 5.24). As a consequence, it became hard to use this desktop for longer than 30 minutes. In order to avoid distracting the user or causing them discomfort, UIs need to be color-friendly, with a soft palette, and the background and icons should be transparent and not overwhelming.

When system performance grew and acquired more capabilities (e.g., detail and higher-resolution icons), computers started to use full color in their UIs (Figure 5.25). By 1997, the Mac OS had begun using gradients and colors that

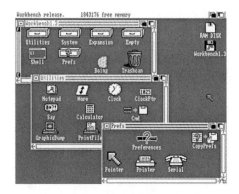

Figure 5.24

Workbench, an OS GUI.

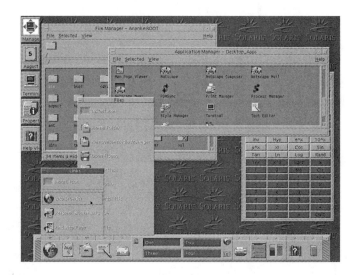

Figure 5.25

Other computer systems entered the market in the 1990s, in this case, Solaris.

appealed to the user because of their realism. In 2001, Mac OS underwent a radical change, into 3D, virtually drawn icons that were as realistic as possible. Meanwhile, Windows kept its icons more like illustrations, rather than 3D versions.

By the 2010s, all Mac OS icons had become 2D, resulting in a more cohesive look (Figure 5.26). The same style spread to Windows 8 as well.

The evolution of icons is not only technological but has also changed people's ways of thinking and how they to react to icons. People in the 1980s were more patient because computers were slower and had limited screen sizes. Nowadays, however, users are more impatient and want to access UIs rapidly, whether on their tablets, desktops, or even watches or glasses. Icons in interfaces have

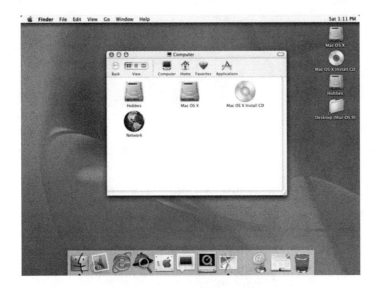

Figure 5.26

Mac OS from 2010.

Figure 5.27

In 2015, many operating systems began to simplify their icons, resulting in a more cohesive and easy-to-manage system.

evolved rapidly, and due to wearable UIs there are significantly fewer limitations (Figure 5.27).

The augmented reality of icons in Google Glass and our interactions with them are incredibly accessible because the icons are monochromatic. As such, visibility is guaranteed regardless of the user's location, and the size of the icons is not distracting (Figures 5.28 and 5.29).

Figure 5.28

Google Glass's OS provides the user with easily accessible main icons in order to enable them to enter apps in the UI.

Figure 5.29

Google Glass responds to situations and interacts with the user.

Figure 5.30

The Apple Watch.

Meanwhile, a completely different approach is the Apple Watch, which has changed the way we think about watches (Figure 5.30). Such devices enable the user to access smaller icons and other types of applications that may be geared toward health, fitness, or other personal needs.

The Present and Future of Icons and Tools

The Noun Project is an icon-sharing space that helps provide designers with icons and also inspiration. In addition, a related project, called *Lingo*, organizes designers' visual libraries on their computer and categorizes everything, making it extremely easy to find icons or any type of image needed for a project. Instead of wasting time searching for an image, designers can instead spend more time choosing the right icons. The interface is extremely friendly and easy to use.

The Noun Project

Based in Los Angeles, the Noun Project is an expanding library that provides free and unlimited downloadable icons (Figure 5.31). To visit this database, go to http://thenounproject.com.

Figure 5.31

The Noun Project website. (Courtesy of Noun Project.)

Lingo

Created by the Noun Project, this is a helpful software tool that manages icons with previous visual access to anything a designer is using when creating an interface (Figure 5.32). On the right side of the screen, the information about the icon set is from the Noun Project.

Figure 5.32

Lingo software. (Courtesy of Youtube.)

Creating Icons

If you are a visual designer planning to customize your icons, it is recommended that you note the number of icons you need to create during the sketch process so that you can effectively balance your time between creating the layout and the icons.

Ensure there is enough time to do both. If you don't see yourself having enough time, it would be best for you to investigate libraries, including the Noun Project, that have beautiful icons. Moreover, if you need icons that are geared solely to the product you are creating, then you can hire an illustrator who is skilled at icon design. Regardless of your decision, below is a useful set of steps to follow when creating icons.

Brainstorming

Start by creating a mind map and by sketching, as this will help you organize your ideas and enable you to determine how many icons you need.

Ask the following questions:

- What is the purpose of the icon(s)?
- What does it/do they symbolize?

Create a list of words that are related to the icons:

- Are there any competitors? List them.

Create imagery of other icons or photos that will help inspire you to start creating the icons. If the icons you are creating were never created before, you have more freedom and fewer restrictions.

Step 1: Sketching

In the sketching process, it is strongly suggested that designers use gridded paper to create their icons. It is a good idea to use pencils, as this will allow changes to be made to the sketch (Figure 5.33). Do not stop after your first idea, even if it is a good one, but start exploring, creating more versions until you think you have exhausted your brain's sense of innovation with your sketches. At that point, you are ready to start digitizing.

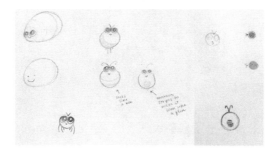

Figure 5.33

Sketching an icon. (Courtesy of Carmella Pombuena.)

The Grid

Whether working digitally or on paper, it is essential that you use a grid (Figure 5.34). Many grid options exist, and the ones below are a few examples that will help you to start thinking about how you want to begin your first sketches.

	ldpi (120 dpi) (Low-density screen)	mdpi (160 dpi) (Medium-density screen)	hdpi (240 dpi) (High-density screen)	xhdpi (320 dpi) (Extra-high-density screen)
Launcher icon size	36 × 36 px	48 × 48 px	72 × 72 px	96 × 96 px

Figure 5.34

Using the human design guidelines for Android interfaces will help create an accurate icon for this type of interface. (Courtesy of Android Developers, Launcher Icons, 2016, https://developer.android.com/guide/practices/ui_guidelines/icon_design_launcher.html.)

Step 2: Scanning

Once you have sketched your image, you will need to scan it to a digital file, which can then be refined and edited (Figure 5.35). For this, you will need image-editing software like Adobe Photoshop. Once the image is clear, it will be easy to trace the image once transferred to Adobe Illustrator, where the icon may be drawn.

Figure 5.35

Scan your sketches.

Step 3: Tracing by Drawing the Icon

Digitizing

Digital drawing tablets are very helpful even during the sketching process, because the digitizer pen is pressure-sensitive and so can be manipulated in the same way as a regular pen, maybe even more so. Drawing tablets usually allow users to erase and make edits at any time, and as such they might be a better option for UI designers (Figure 5.36).

Designers who do not have access to a drawing tablet can still use their computers, drawing and tracing with the mouse or the trackpad to good effect.

Figure 5.36

Digital work.

Step 4: Refine the Edges and Refine the Number of Vector Points in the Drawing

Step 5: Add Color and Hierarchy within the Space

It is likely that you will need to create a brand icon for an application, a logo for a website, or some type of new or rebranded identity for the interface you are creating. It is incredibly important to determine color palettes prior to this stage (Figure 5.37).

When creating a new version of a common icon, make sure that the design remains simple; avoid creating an image that will confuse the user. Keep in mind that he or she will be testing the app, website, or software. If it is ambiguous, the designer will need to start all over again, wasting time and money invested in the project. From the beginning, the UI designer needs to know the limitations and branding guidelines, among other things, in order to create a successful interface (Figure 5.38).

Creating a brand identity icon for the app Flee, including names (Figure 5.39).

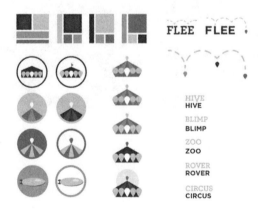

Figure 5.37

Icon system branding digital versions and studies.

5. Typography, Icons, and User Legibility

Figure 5.38

Final logo.

Figure 5.39

Brand identity guide of the app, including typography and color.

Initially, the app did not have a name, and so various options were considered via a study of names and colors, as presented above. Once the name *Flee* was decided upon, it was possible to design an icon for the app.

Icon Guidelines

Android Design: https://developer.android.com/design/index.html
Microsoft Design: https://developer.microsoft.com/en-us/windows/desktop/design

Apple
OS X Human Interface Guidelines: https://developer.apple.com/library/mac/documentation/UserExperience/Conceptual/OSXHIGuidelines/Designing.html#//apple_ref/doc/uid/20000957-CH87-SW1 (Figure 5.40).

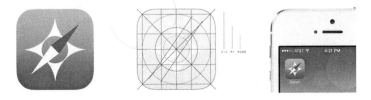

Figure 5.40

Icon for Safari: Apple example.

User Legibility

Earlier in this chapter, we discussed typography and icons, which have a lot in common. Both are used to communicate a message to the user through letterforms and icons, and both have come a long way since the beginning of the UI, when the first screen was a very low 606w × 808h pixel resolution. Although its GUI was not commercialized, the Apple Lisa had a resolution of 720w × 360h. By contrast, the smallest MacBook Pro has a resolution of 2560w × 1600h. Thus, the resolution and quality of pixels have drastically changed and evolved and, in doing so, have altered over time the ratio of how letters and icons are seen on the interface. Therefore, guidance concerning legibility is constantly evolving and transforming along with technology's constant state of flux. The future will likely witness increasingly high resolutions for the web, apps, software, and others.

Perception

Typefaces and icons are at least 85% of most interfaces, and therefore they have a large impact on our positive or negative perceptions. Thousands of studies have been conducted in testing labs all over the world, designed to help us to understand this large percentage better and to ascertain what users like and dislike in interfaces in terms of legibility. The following are a selection of such studies, chosen because they directly concern user legibility.

Case 1: The New York Times (A Confidence Study)

The *New York Times* conducted a study in which thousands of its readers were exposed to articles that were identical in content but presented in different typefaces: Baskerville, Comic Sans, Computer Modern, Georgia, Helvetica, and Trebuchet. The goal of the study was to ascertain which typeface inspired more confidence in the reader. According to the 40,000 readers who participated, Baskerville generated the most trust (Morris, 2012). By contrast, Georgia did not make a good impression, and Comic Sans caused a sense of disregard (Figure 5.41). The results of this study reveal that it is extremely important to pay attention to the layout and organization of the type used, including spacing, typeface style, and more. But testing and interpreting

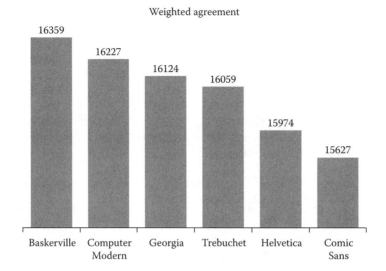

Weighted agreement

Figure 5.41

Infographic showing user preference for typeface. (Courtesy of *The New York Times*, 2012. Available at https://opinionator.blogs.nytimes.com/2012/08/08/hear-all-ye-people-hearken-o-earth/?_r=0.)

how users react to the product is just as important in order to gauge success. Designers are not perfect and must rely on user feedback to inform their work. Therefore, the context of the content is just as important as the choices of the users when it comes to overall testing.

Case 2: Student Typeface Papers (Non-UI Study)

Over a period of six semesters, a student wrote 52 essays. He observed that his grades improved toward the end, yet he reflected that he hadn't done anything to change his routine or anything that he thought would have resulted in greater success. The only thing he had changed was to replace his earlier use of Times New Roman and Trebuchet with Georgia. Reflecting back on his grades, he was able to observe that Trebuchet in particular inspired a negative reaction in the grader.

The Influence of User Testing

The only way to determine whether the legibility of the visual interface design is working is through testing, not just once, but several times, as needed. This process varies from project to project, and there is no special formula. It is important for the researcher to work diligently and closely with the interface designer on revisions of typography and iconography. For further information on user testing, see Chapter 13.

This area is one of the newest areas of study in the field of human-centered design. Since the release of the Xerox Alto, interfaces have not changed drastically, particularly in relation to typefaces and icons. User testing is a vital part of the prototyping process and should be included from the outset in order to ensure a successful interface.

The Importance of Knowing, Understanding, and Applying Studies and Statistics

Studies have been conducted to help us understand more about legibility. In 2008, Harald Weinreich and Jakob Nielsen researched web pages and measured page views from 25 different users. Of a total of 45,237 page views, only 20% of the text was read most of the time.

Outcomes of Several Research Studies

- Low contrast in the layout, small type, and small amount of leading are some of the largest complaints.
- Health and age affect legibility, especially in people over 40 years old and even more so in those over 60. In addition, 60% of Americans use corrective lenses.
- According to the World Health Organization, 246 million people need corrective lenses, and 39 million are blind (WHO, 2016).

Being able to understand the user in depth, including their vision health, is incredibly important when creating visual interfaces. Some interfaces have created modes for users who are color blind, partially sighted, or totally blind. It is extremely important to keep options for such users available during the creation process.

Spaces and Environments

Interfaces are accessed from various environments and on different screen types, and while we cannot control all of this information, we can provide options for legibility. For example, a white or light, bright background would benefit users in dark environments, or the user may prefer a darker tone for the background. It is important to give users such options from which to choose, because not everyone will access the information in the same way. In addition, for people who are blind, it is important to add audio to the interface.

Images and Types

The combination of both images and type creates a very high level of hierarchy, usually right after the navigation. It is important to spend the time to create visually appealing designs that attract the attention of the user and help him or her to understand the nature of a specific section.

Best Typeface Size for Screen Copy

Using 16 px for body copy is very important when designing for a screen, especially for the web. Taking into account the distance from the screen, 16 px seems to be the same size when printed and placed at the same distance. Obviously,

Reading statistic	Font size		
	Small	Medium	Large
1st-Pass speed (char/s)	41.1 (9.5)	44.6 (13)	46.3 (13)
Regression rate (reg/s)	0.39 (0.20)	0.40 (0.19)	0.38 (0.16)
Total sweep time (s)	3.48 (1.3)	4.22 (1.2)	4.66 (1.1)
Fraction re-read (%)	30.6 (15)	30.0 (14)	28.2 (15)
Saccade length (char)	11.0 (2.3)	10.8 (2.8)	10.4 (2.7)
Fixation duration (ms)	281 (36)	261 (47)	239 (22)
Retention (% correct)	89.2 (16)	90.1 (18)	88.9 (16)

Figure 5.42

Table study showing font size preferences for reading. (Courtesy of *The New York Times*, 2012. Available at https://opinionator.blogs.nytimes.com/2012/08/08/hear-all-ye-people-hearken-o-earth/?_r=0.)

this could vary slightly by typeface, because the x-heights of typefaces vary (Figure 5.42). However, overall the difference will not be very great.

Another study that supports this argument was conducted at Payame Noor University in Iran, involving a joint eye-tracking study with IBM/Google. The research demonstrated that reading speed increases with typeface size.

These studies encourage interface designers to take into consideration what users need, not what the designer wants.

Reading Patterns

Many applications geared to various sizes have been developed, ranging from those that allow writing an email to apps that allow the user to text. All these forms of reading also encourage a behavioral pattern in the user. For example, a person will not be able to write or read a long email in only a few minutes, so sitting at a desktop for such tasks may be the best option. By contrast, a tweet or a text has a completely different purpose, and the user can read and respond in seconds to such communications. Therefore, there are two means of typographic communication: (1) formal, diplomatic, and professional and (2) informal and fast.

Condensed Typefaces: A Warning

The use of condensed typefaces in interfaces should be limited because of legibility issues. The more condensed the typeface is, the more likely it is that legibility problems will arise. It is best to look into wider letterforms when exploring typefaces.

Responsiveness

Responsiveness began with the changing screen sizes that came with the advent of the iPhone, tablets, and wearables. Typography and legibility are completely different on all types of screens. Several human factors must be considered, including human anatomy and cognitive processes. Therefore, given that typography is a medium of communication, the most essential parts to consider are size, spacing, letters, words, sentences, leading, type style, and column width. Due to their individual sizes, every device will need to have a different view, which includes changing the essential parts of the typography in the interface. Apps such as Apple iTunes have an interface that is 70% typographic because it contains information about music that users want to hear. Users can listen to music via various devices, including a desktop or an Apple Watch, but all of them have different sizes, so the purpose of the interface must shift from one to the other. If a user accesses iTunes from their desktop, he or she will probably have more time to view the navigation and will see much more. Meanwhile, the Apple Watch user can access music with more freedom, doing so while jogging, for example. Overall, these devices have different purposes, and the typography is therefore accessed differently and according to human factors. The distance of the eyes to the application will vary from device to device, for instance. Therefore, it is extremely important to perform user testing in order to make good decisions when arranging the type for a UI.

Flexibility and Simplicity

When going to a restaurant and paying for a dish, a customer expects to receive an item that they like. If the restaurant does not have the flexibility to ensure this, the patron will probably not return, especially if there are food allergies involved. It is vital to apply the simple rule of flexibility in interfaces, because billions of users access apps, websites, and computers worldwide. Providing the flexibility to offer a different language, for example, is incredibly helpful.

One study found that 94% of users provided comments on the layout of a UI, including typography, color, and the complexity of the website interface. Meanwhile, only 6% provided feedback on content. Poor design showed a lack of trust and led to rejection.

All these aspects push us to become more aware of the decisions that are made from the outset of our prototypes. Regarding simplicity, the more accessible the content is, the easier it will be for the user to interact with the interface. Simplicity means having order in the hierarchy, transparent navigation, and much more. Flexibility causes the user to feel more deeply connected, because not only is he or she retrieving information but also the interface is making it more accessible according to his or her needs.

For example, a user may encounter an app that strains the eyes because the contrast is too dark or because the user has vision problems. If the app has accessibility options to change the contrast of the background and foreground, then it should be easy for the user to remedy this problem, which increases the likelihood of repeated use.

Users want to feel they can control the interface and enjoy using it at the same time. This can be achieved by changing backgrounds, typefaces, sizes, and so on. Flexible options should be available to the user. Another example is an elderly person who wants to access his or her smartphone but can't see the icons because they are too small. As such, there should be an option to change the size of the icons in line with an awareness that not everyone has perfect vision.

Overall, it is impossible to please everyone. At the same time, it is important to offer as many options as possible to enable people to comfortably use your interfaces.

Ownership

When someone purchases an interface with the intention of using it on a daily basis, options and flexibility are vital. Increased time spent with the interface leads a user to enjoy it. This leads to a sense of ownership, which has existed since the Apple Lisa. People were willing to pay $10,000 dollars for a Lisa despite its 1 MB capacity. They wanted to own the device in order to interact with it and be able to perform previously impossible tasks, such as word processing and playing computer games. They were also able to enjoy sitting at the computer and using the keyboard and mouse. Every piece of hardware or software has a responsibility to serve this broad purpose of pleasing its user.

Today, users want to have visual interactive experiences with their icons, menus, typography, and images. Because product experience is competitive, innovation in relation to the visual experience is essential.

Moods

Typography clearly impacts the mood of the reader or user. When choosing a typeface or typefaces for an interface, it is incredibly important to get to know the personality of the typeface(s), because typography is an active and living language that communicates directly with the user. If the mood or personality of the typeface does not appeal to the majority of users, which can be ascertained by tests, then it is very important to keep exploring other typefaces. The voice and body of the interface are the typography and icons, and if we spend time editing and correcting all the visual grammar of the content, then the interface will succeed and the user's cognitive performance will also improve.

Helpful Tools

Readability is extremely important. There are already tools to help users.

1. Readability app: https://www.readability.com/
   This application is very helpful for accessing content on the web. The reader is able to block ads or anything that does not relate to the desired content, which thus becomes very simple, as seen in Figures 5.43 and 5.44.
2. Legibility app
   This app allows anyone to test type settings, including spacing, leading, visibility distance, contrast, 3D options, and even open type features.

Figure 5.43

Before using the Readability app (https://www.readability.com/).

Figure 5.44

With the Readability app.

The Evolution of Typography and Icons

As we progress in the development and creation of smarter interfaces, we need to maintain focus on user needs. No matter how evolved technology becomes, what will always be important is the user or reader and how they will access the information in a stress-free manner. Though we cannot please everyone, there is an incredible need to take legibility seriously and explore other ways in which layouts can increase visibility (Figures 5.45 through 5.47).

Websites have their own methods of navigation and exploration, which thus differ from apps and software systems. Therefore, it is important to create a set of helpful standards to manage all these platforms. Again, some rules will not serve everyone, but it is important to help create a foundation. For example, the article earlier in this chapter concerning the 16 px font-size rule for web legibility can be used and applied by any designer to their own work.

Navigation is incredibly important on the web. Hierarchy is needed to show that there is a link that can be opened anytime. Web pages need to be flexible,

Figure 5.45

Legibility Inspector.

Figure 5.46

Contrast 70.7%, pixelation 7 px.

Figure 5.47

Vision 63.73 ft, overglow 1.17, pixelation 0 px, contrast 70.7%.

enabling a nonlinear reading process instead of forcing readers to skim through the page in search of relevant content.

Meanwhile, wearables and small devices are limited in size but still require large text sizes (16 px), as well as leading and bold weights, because of the user's movement that comes with their portability. The smaller the interface, the stronger contrast is needed and the more direct the icons and typography need to be.

Drawing the Line

As interface designers, our job is to please the user, but we cannot do so by breaking typographic design rules that are extremely important. Most users are not visually or esthetically trained, and it is important for us to guide them through the limitations. For example, imagine you are designing an app that you share with a future user to test its potential success, but she doesn't like the typeface, preferring Comic Sans because, she says, she feels comfortable reading it. In that case, bearing in mind the studies that have shown the inappropriateness of that typeface, it is your duty as an interface designer to listen to the test user but also to teach her that there are other beautiful typefaces out there that she may also enjoy.

References

Android Developers. 2016. Launcher Icons | Accessed July 31, 2016. https://developer.android.com/guide/practices/ui_guidelines/icon_design_launcher.html.

Bay, Susanne, and Ziefle, Martina. 2005. Children using cellular phones: The effects of shortcomings in user interface design. *Human Factors* 47(1): 158–68.

Bosler, Denise. 2012. *Mastering Type: The Essential Guide to Typography for Print and Web Design*. HOW Books, Blue Ash, OH.

Boyarski, Dan, Boyarski, Dan, Neuwirth, Christine, Forlizzi, Jodi, Regli, and Susan Harkness. 1998. A Study of Fonts Designed for Screen Display. In *Proceedings of the SIGCHI Conference on Human Factors in Computing Systems—CHI'98*. doi:10.1145/274644.274658. Los Angeles, California, USA — April 18–23. ACM Press/Addison-Wesley Publishing Co. New York.

Chai, Xinyu, Yu, Wei, Wang, Jia, Zhao, Ying, Cai, Changsi, and Ren, Qiushi. 2007. Recognition of pixelized chinese Characters using simulated prosthetic vision. *Artificial Organs* 31(3): 175–82.

Cordova, Viviana. 2012. *Web Typography: A Handbook for Graphic Designers*. Createspace Independent Pub, North Charleston, SC.

Covert, Adrian. 2014. Why Apple's New Font Won't Work On Your Desktop. *Co. Design*. June 3. Accessed April 21, 2017. http://www.fastcodesign.com/3031432/why-apples-new-font-wont-work-on-your-desktop.

Damieng.com. Accessed July 31, 2016. https://images.damieng.com/fonts/converted/AltoMono.png.

Designhistory. 2016. Early Technologies of Digital Type. Accessed July 31, 2016. http://www.designhistory.org/Digital_Revolution_pages/EarlyDigType.html.

Hoefler & Co. 2016. Combining Fonts | Accessed July 31, 2016. http://www.typography.com/techniques/index.php.

Hoefler & Co. 2016. Forza Fonts | Accessed July 31, 2016. http://www.typography.com/fonts/forza/styles/screensmart/.

Hoefler & Co. 2016. Whitney Fonts | Accessed July 31, 2016. http://www.typography.com/fonts/whitney/styles/screensmart/.

Process Type Foundry. 2016. Elena Font Family | Accessed July 31, 2016. http://processtypefoundry.com/fonts/elena/.

Isotype Revisited. 2016a. | From Hieroglyphics to Isotype. Accessed July 31, 2016. http://isotyperevisited.org/2009/09/from-hieroglyphics-to-isotype.html.

Isotype Revisited. 2016b. | *Isotype* "Picture Dictionary." Accessed July 31, 2016. http://isotyperevisited.org/2009/09/isotype-picture-dictionary-1.html.

Lupton, Ellen, and Maryland Institute College of Art. 2014. *Type on Screen: A Critical Guide for Designers, Writers, Developers, and Students*. Chronicle Books, San Francisco, CA.

Morris, E. 2012. Hear, All Ye People; Hearken, O Earth (Part 1). Accessed July 31, 2016. http://opinionator.blogs.nytimes.com/2012/08/08/hear-all-ye-people-hearken-o-earth/?_r=0.

Noun Project. 2016. *Noun Project*. Accessed July 31, 2016. https://thenounproject.com.

Pamental, Jason. 2014. *Responsive Typography: Using Type Well on the Web*. O'Reilly Media, Inc, Sebastopol, CA.

Support Apple. 2017. Accessed June 13, 2017. https://support.apple.com/en-us/HT200553.

This Was The First Computer Font. 2016. *Pinterest*. Accessed July 31, 2016. https://www.pinterest.com/pin/238831586459213533/.

Typotheque: Fedra Mono Screen Font Family. 2016. Accessed July 31, 2016. https://www.typotheque.com/fonts/fedra_mono_screen.

Typotheque: Font Hinting by Peter Biľak. 2016. Accessed July 31, 2016. https://www.typotheque.com/articles/hinting.

Typotheque: Vita Font Family. 2016. Accessed July 31, 2016. https://www.typotheque.com/fonts/vita.

Visual Representation: The Encyclopedia of Human-Computer Interaction, 2nd Ed. 2016. *The Interaction Design Foundation*. Accessed July 31, 2016. https://www.interaction-design.org/literature/book/the-encyclopedia-of-human-computer-interaction-2nd-ed/visual-representation.

Web Design Is 95% Typography | iA. 2016. Accessed July 31, 2016. https://ia.net/know-how/the-web-is-all-about-typography-period.

WHO, Visual Impairment and Blindness. 2016, February. World Health Organization. Accessed April 21, 2017. http://www.reuters.com/article/us-health-qualityoflife-vision-impairmen-idUSKCN0RH2KT20150917.

Youtube. 2016. *Affinity Designer Tutorial—Organising Assets Using Lingo*. Accessed April 21, 2017. https://www.youtube.com/watch?v=W3fBSB6nWgE.

6

Image Making

Images in interfaces are made of pixels varying in size and resolution. The evolution of digital images did not begin with the graphical user interface (GUI). Images became an important part of the GUI with the Apple Lisa, but only in monochrome and at an extremely low resolution. Over time, images have evolved, with increasing numbers of pixels as humans seek higher resolutions to get closer and closer to reality.

History of the Pixel and Its Influence

The history of the pixel began right after the innovation of color television. At that time, the pixel had various names, such as *pix*. Fred Crockett Billingsley, who dedicated his life to the research of digital imaging, wrote the first papers that used the word *pixel*, an abbreviation of *picture element* (Figure 6.1). The use of computer monitors in the early 1970s was still very new in the scientific and business communities, but once it spread and the number of pixels increased compared with television, new horizons and fields of research were created, such as digital imaging, in both computer science and the arts.

Figure 6.1

Fred Crockett Billingsley (1921–2002). He is behind the oscilloscope in the Image Processing Lab at Jet Propulsion Laboratory (JPL) with technician George Peterson and the Link Video–Film Converter. Photo included in both of Billingsley's 1965 International Society of Optics and Photonics (SPIE) papers.

A pixel is the smallest piece of an image that a computer can display onscreen and through printing on paper. Pixels are small squares that capture light in red, green, and blue. The evolution of resolution has allowed more and more pixels in a screen, which has created high-resolution quality in various devices, including projectors. Pixels are the foundation of color for all types of screens—not only for computers, but also for cameras, signage, and much more.

Various types of display use pixels, including cathode ray tube (almost obsolete), plasma, organic light-emitting diode, and liquid crystal displays. Over time, pixels have become smaller and smaller, enabling crisper definition of images and everything else in computer interfaces.

Resolution

Resolution, the quality of an image, is defined by the number of pixels in that image. More pixels make an image seem more real to our eyes, so resolution is constantly evolving. Though there is a wide range of resolutions and displays, we concentrate here on the most-used ones (Figures 6.2–6.4).

According to several statistics ("Screen Resolution Statistics" 2016), the resolution that has become most standard and popular since 2012 is 1366 × 768, overtaking 1024 × 768. Screen sizes will constantly change, so we must update our knowledge of which sizes we should design to, whether for web or app interfaces. Concerning images, we must know that resolutions and screens are always improving, remembering that many things influence the size of the designed interface. It is extremely important to discover all such device attributes before sketching out or even thinking about the layout, as it is impossible to know what should be in an interface without the correct size. Moreover, if the interface is geared solely to one type of device, such as Android smartphones, the design will be a bit easier. Regardless of the simplicity (one device) or complexity (several devices), it is necessary to understand the human-centered design guidelines for each type of device, which most likely have different operating systems. As mentioned in previous chapters, it is important to keep in touch with the developer to come to an agreement regarding technical restrictions that may affect your design.

Types of Pixels

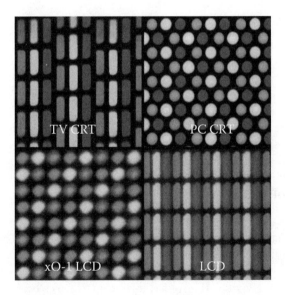

Figure 6.2

Types of screen pixels straight from screens. (Courtesy of Pengo, 2016, https://commons.wikimedia.org/wiki/File:Pixel_geometry_01_Pengo.jpg.)

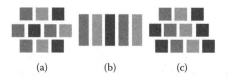

(a)　　　　(b)　　　　(c)

Figure 6.3

There are three types of pixels used by various types of screens: (a) triangular, (b) stripes, and (c) diagonal. Most of the time, we cannot see the shape of the pixels, because they are so small.

72 PPI ORIGINAL IMAGE　　　　300 PPI LARGER IMAGE

Figure 6.4

Icon from ULock App created by Andrea Cervantes Medina and Oluwasola Awojoodu. This image has been resized from the original size of 72 ppi to a larger version of 300 ppi, which has become distorted.

1. All images in interfaces should have a minimum resolution of 72 ppi (pixels per inch). The design guidelines for every device will require double, triple, or more versions of images in resolutions higher than 72 ppi to satisfy devices' different resolutions. Please follow these guidelines.

2. When resizing images, unless it has a particular function and purpose, do not enlarge a 72 ppi image, because it will look pixelated, meaning you can see the pixels that form the image.

Formats

PNG, which stands for *Portable Networks Graphic*, is used largely for images on the web and in apps.

- PNG 8 is low resolution, only allowing up to 256 colors.
- PNG 24 is true color, with higher resolution than 256 colors.
- PNG 32 is true color resolution with more than 256 colors and with transparency of various degrees.

GIF, which stands for *Graphics Interchange Format,* is more limited than PNG, but it also allows animation within an image. GIF compresses images to a smaller file size, while at the same time allowing animation (ongoing, playing just once, twice, or an arbitrary number of times). Usually, we can create GIF animations in Photoshop. Transparency is available in GIF, but it is not the best in quality unless the graphic is geometric and only has one or two colors. There are options in Photoshop to convert to GIF 32, 64, and 128 with the options of dithered, not dithered, and GIF restrictive.

JPEG files might not display with good quality on some devices and for some interfaces. It is important to test and ask the developer for feedback. Most likely, this file type is solely recommended for photographic images.

Make sure to create a folder for your images. Do not save your images everywhere, because you will waste your time looking for them.

Overall, the file types described above provide many options for different types of images. It is extremely important to become efficient in managing the sizes of images early in the process so that you get some idea of how much space they will take. Share this information with the developer, as well, so they can highlight any limitations for you, whether the image is for an operating system, app, or website.

Graphic versus Photographic

Graphic images are usually part of the interface design itself, including navigational icons, illustrations, or even abstract color shapes. Such images are usually smaller in file size compared with photographs, because they use fewer colors and have less detail, while photographs are extremely detailed even if monochromatic. Images must be made at various stages of the interface prototyping process, from paper to digital.

Cropping a Photograph

When cropping a photograph to place in the interface, it is extremely important to follow the rule of thirds, which breaks the space or canvas into three individual spaces, both vertical and horizontal. This grid provides a skeleton around which the image should be arranged. I do not suggest you break this rule, but, if you do, you need to be aware that you are breaking it. The rule of thirds is used in many fields, including design. The thirds do not have any particular dimensions; what matters is that the chosen images use and match the grid.

Cameras

If you are taking photos for the interface yourself, most cameras and even many smartphones with cameras have a rule of thirds setting as an option when taking a picture (Figure 6.5). If you are collecting images this way, I encourage you to try it. It will make editing in Photoshop or any other imaging software much easier.

Figure 6.5

Rule of thirds applied in an image. (Courtesy of Rule of Thirds in Photography, 2006, *Digital Photography School*, http://digital-photography-school.com/rule-of-thirds/.)

Paper Prototyping Stages

During paper prototyping, any type of images may be drawn directly on paper or printed digitally, including icons. Images can be cut and pasted on top of a paper canvas. This extremely fast process may be done in black and white or in color, all depending on your budget.

Sizing

Images should preferably be saved as 72 dpi, because most screens or projectors use a resolution of 72 dpi or higher. If an image has a resolution of 300 dpi, it is four times larger. This is useless if not required, as it is taking more space and could even crash the website or app or create other problems. Therefore, it is essential to save files as 72 dpi, even if we now have very high screen resolutions. For example, the size of a mobile app usually does not surpass 1 MB; therefore, the typefaces, images, icons, and all other media need to be extremely small to provide space for the code and everything else that the app needs. Images created for a website or desktop application may be larger, but be aware that space is golden when it comes to image sizing.

Images and Layering

It is important to create layers within images to create hierarchy, especially when adding shapes, colors, and text. Many of us should experiment more with overlaying, cropping, changing transparency, or resizing to find the best layout for the images. Experimenting is especially important if the image has type and will be presented in the main sections of the user interface.

Different types of ways to arrange an image or photographs are shown in the Figures 6.6–6.8.

6. Image Making

Gallery

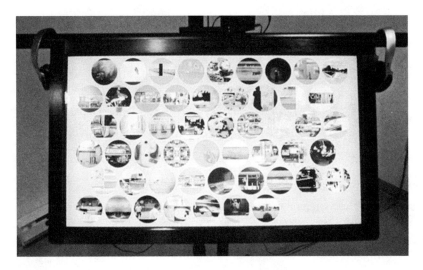

Figure 6.6

Interface showcasing a gallery. (Courtesy of Interactive In-Gallery Video Kiosk for Artist Midi Onodera—Marty Spellerberg, 2016, http://martyspellerberg.com/2011/10/interactivetouchscreen-interface-using-jquery-and-html5-video/.)

Source Image

Background

Figure 6.7

Background image on Apple computers. (Courtesy of Lyons, I., 2016, *ColorSync for Mac OSX*, http://www.computer-darkroom.com/colorsync-display/colorsync_1.htm.)

Informative or Infographic Using Images

Image Transparency

Transparent images may be used as icons, transparent background images, and more (Figures 6.9 and 6.10). Transparent images are usually saved in PNG format.

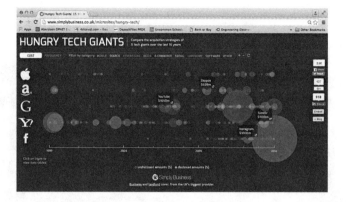

Figure 6.8

Hungry Tech Giants. (Courtesy of Hungry Tech Giants: 15 Years of Tech Acquisitions, 2016, Simply Business, http://www.simplybusiness.co.uk/microsites/hungry-tech/.)

Figure 6.9

Transparent image in Photoshop.

Image as Icon

Figure 6.10

Icon representing Settings.

Animated Image

An animated image can be used as an ad banner, a button, or an icon (Figure 6.11). The example below is a sticker, usually used in text messages and chat apps.

Figure 6.11

Icon in motion. (Courtesy of Animated Stickers Now Available on LINE! Spice Up Chats With Stickers That Will Move You: LINE Official Blog, 2016, *LINE Official Blog*, http://official-blog.line.me/en/archives/1004315501.html.)

The image type best suited for animation is GIF, which accepts animations and is saved as a single image.

Regarding digitization, we need to prepare the images differently for each operating system used on each device, for example iOS, Android, or Windows.

It is very important that you work closely with the developer(s), who will make the app functional. They should give you the exact specifications regarding screen resolution and whether the app is designed, for example, for a desktop system or an Apple or Android phone. Having a good relationship with the developer team is very important for reaching your highest potential and the visual goals you want to achieve with your UI. Communication is key to creating the correct image sizes and layouts. In addition, make sure that the images or icons you create are tested in several stages by future users and not only by the designers and developers of the app. Overall, the process of creating an image should be as transparent as possible to make the decisions and results very clear.

For iOS, the most compatible image file types are JPEG and PNG, and even PDF. For Android, images should be scalable vector graphics (SVG), JPEG, or PNG files. In Windows, it is best to use PNG and JPEG files.

Experimenting with Images

Photoshop software provides many options for editing images. Some instructions for common tasks are below.

Cropping

1. Open Photoshop
2. From the main, top menu, select File > Open. (Select the image from your folders.)

3. From the vertical toolbar on the left, choose the second icon > Rectangular Marquee Tool > select and hold.
4. Then, choose from the Rectangular, Elliptical, Single Row, and Single Column Marquee tools.
5. Select the area of the canvas that you want to crop.
6. Select from the main menu.
7. Open Photoshop > Main Image Select > Crop.
8. The image has now been cropped.

Preparing Images in Grayscale

1. Open Photoshop.
2. From the main, top menu, select File > Open. (Select the image from your folders.)
3. Select Mode > Grayscale.

Preparing Images in Black and White

1. Open Photoshop.
2. From the main, top menu, select File > Open. (Select the image from your folders.)
3. From the main, top menu, select Image: Adjustment > Black and White.

Preparing Images in Color

1. Open Photoshop.
2. From the main, top menu, select File > Open. (Select the image from your folders.)
3. From the main, top menu, select Image: Adjustment. You can choose from 22 adjustment options overall in Photoshop, from Brightness and Contrast to Equalize.

Preparing Images with Patterns (Graphics)

1. Open Photoshop.
2. From the main, top menu, select File > Save for the Web.
3. From the menu, select Save for the Web.
4. On the right side, select Preset > and then select the most convenient option. In this case, PNG might be the strongest option. I encourage you to choose the best quality and the smallest size from among all the options.
5. At the bottom, select Save.
6. A window will pop up, asking in what folder to place the image. Select from the bottom menu > Save.
7. The image has now been saved.

Preparing Bitmap Images

Figure 6.12

Photoshop Option Mode.

When converting an image to a bitmap, it is important to first convert the image to grayscale, whether the image is color or monochrome (Figure 6.12).

If you have layers in your Photoshop file, follow the instructions below; otherwise, skip to the next paragraph.

In your layers window (Windows > Layers), you cannot have more than one layer in use. If you have several layers, use the merge layers option (in the Layers window, select the hamburger menu on the right, and then from the drop-down menu select Merge layers).

Once you've followed this step, do the following (Figure 6.13):

1. Open Photoshop.
2. From the main menu, select Image > Mode > Bitmap.
3. After selecting Bitmap, a window will pop up showing that every inch or centimeter (selected in the drop-down menu) of the image has 72 dpi. You can reduce or increase this according to your preferences. The lower the number, the more abstract and smaller the image will become.

Figure 6.13

Photoshop Bitmap dialog box.

4. From the Method drop-down menu, choose 50% Threshold, Pattern Dither, Diffusion Dither, Halftone Screen, or Custom Pattern (Figure 6.14). These options will help you reach the goal you want to accomplish with your images.

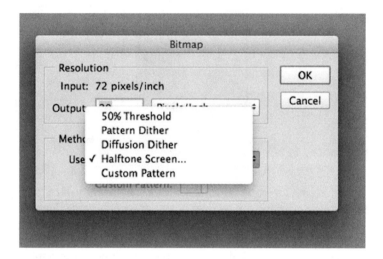

Figure 6.14

Photoshop Bitmap method options.

Before and after Image Example

Preparing Images as Monotone, Duotone, Tritone, Quadtone, or Custom

When you want to convert an image to a monotone, duotone, tritone, quad-tone, or a custom image with a set number of colors, it is important to first convert to grayscale (see method above), whether the image is color or mono-chrome (Figure 6.15).

1. Open Photoshop, then select File > Open (open the image).
2. From the main menu, select Image > Mode > Grayscale.
   If you cannot change the image to grayscale, you might have layers in your Photoshop file. If you were able to change the image to grayscale, skip the next paragraph.
   In your layers window (Windows > Layers), you cannot have more than one layer in use. If you have several layers, use the merge layers option (in the Layers window, select the hamburger menu on the right, and then from the drop-down menu select > Merge layers).
   Once you've changed the image to grayscale, do the following.
3. Select from the main menu Image > Mode > Duotone.

Figure 6.15

Photoshop duotone options.

4. Once the pop-up menu for Duotone appears, select from the options in the window.
5. Under the Preset menu, the Custom option allows you to select the colors that will work only for duotone.

The Type drop-down menu gives you four options: Monotone, Duotone, Tritone, and Quadtone (Figures 6.16–6.19).

1. Monotone will allow you to add only one color to your grayscale image.
2. Duotone will allow you to add two colors to your grayscale image.
3. Tritone will allow you to add three colors to your grayscale image.
4. Quadtone will allow you to add four colors to your grayscale image.

Figure 6.16

Photoshop monotone options.

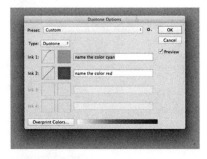

Figure 6.17

Photoshop duotone options.

Figure 6.18

Photoshop tritone options.

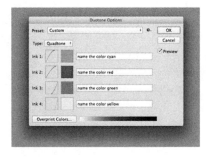

Figure 6.19

Photoshop quadtone options.

Halftone

You can create a halftone image from any image, whether color, black and white, or grayscale (Figure 6.20).

1. Open the file in Photoshop.
2. Go to the main menu and select Filter > Pixelate > Color Halftone.

Figure 6.20

Photoshop halftone options.

3. The Halftone window will appear.

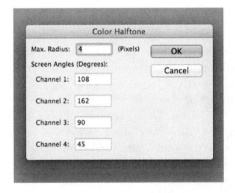

Figure 6.21

Photoshop halftone radius.

In this window, the minimum radius is 4 px and the maximum is 127. You can edit the values of the angles for each of the four channels (Figure 6.21).

How to Prepare Images for Interfaces (Size and Resolution)

1. Open Photoshop and go to File > Open.
2. Once the file is open, check the file size by going to the main menu and selecting Image > Image Size.
3. The pop-up window will present many options. Inside Dimensions, you can change the size, if needed, or add a resolution. Once you've made the necessary changes, select OK (Figure 6.22).

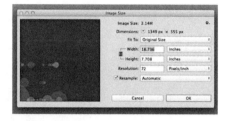

Figure 6.22

Photoshop image size settings.

Limitations and Guidelines

The range of sizes and options for images in interfaces for the web, apps, and other types of software is very broad. Therefore, it is best to follow the guidelines, limitations, and rules for each device or browser. For great examples of studies of various devices, please visit Chapters 14 through 16.

References

Animated Stickers Now Available on LINE! Spice Up Chats With Stickers That Will Move You: LINE Official Blog. 2016. *LINE Official Blog.* Accessed August 1, 2016. http://official-blog.line.me/en/archives/1004315501.html.

Hungry Tech Giants: 15 Years of Tech Acquisitions. 2016. *Simply Business.* Accessed August 1, 2016. http://www.simplybusiness.co.uk/microsites/hungry-tech/.

Interactive In-Gallery Video Kiosk for Artist Midi Onodera—Marty Spellerberg. 2016. Accessed August 1, 2016. http://martyspellerberg.com/2011/10/interactive-touchscreen-interface-using-jquery-and-html5-video/.

Lyons, Ian. 2016. *ColorSync for Mac OSX.* Accessed August 1, 2016. http://www.computer-darkroom.com/colorsync-display/colorsync_1.htm.

Pixel Geometry, Wikipedia. 2016. Accessed August 1, 2016. https://en.wikipedia.org/wiki/Pixel_geometry#/media/File:Pixel_geometry_01_Pengo.jpg.

Rule of Thirds in Photography. 2006. *Digital Photography School.* May 2. Accessed April 21, 2017. http://digital-photography-school.com/rule-of-thirds/.

Screen Resolution Statistics. 2016. Accessed August 1, 2016. http://www.rapidtables.com/web/dev/screen-resolution-statistics.htm.

7

Visual Hierarchy

All levels of hierarchy within any UI must be transparent to allow the user to interact with it comfortably. Visual hierarchy and the patterns underlying it form the core of the UI.

Layers

Layers are bits and pieces of a larger image. When cooking, ingredients have to be added in the right order for the meal to be delicious. Layers are the same; if not in order, the image will be displeasing to the eye, and the presented information will be incoherent. Therefore, during sketching, the designer must correctly layer the structure of an interface. For example, where should the main navigation go? What about the text? Where will copyrights and branding be applied? These and many other components create an interactive image, which is the interface.

Visual Hierarchy

Visual hierarchy concerns the range of levels in which every part of the UI is placed. Every level has a purpose and priority. For example, the background of a UI is always set behind, which is its purpose.

As another example, if there is a main menu located all the way at the top, should it be present there all the time? Such questions should be answered during the process of sketching and early prototyping. For more information on that topic, see Chapter 3.

Organizing the hierarchy of the interface becomes more complex once images and content become involved. The way we interact with websites or apps makes what the user sees first incredibly important. If a user tries to login but the UI has no menu or easy steps for doing so at once, the UI has already failed. Therefore, it is important to keep making adjustments according to users' needs. For example, a UI meant for toddlers must be extremely simple, because toddlers have few capabilities to interact with the screen or to read large amounts of text. The layers in such a UI should thus be extremely clear and direct, and it would also be important to test toddlers from the stage of paper prototyping. More generally, UI designers should invite user testers into the UI, analyzing these tests from the most important to the least important parts of the UI.

Designing a House

Consider the design of a house. We enter the house through the front door, and hallways, corridors, and stairs lead us into various rooms, some of which might be more important than others, such as the kitchen, living room, bathroom, or bedrooms. Any person building a house will have certain priorities. So, too, in UI design will every client have priorities. At the end of the day, the most important person in the whole design process is the user, not the client, since the user will be accessing the app or website frequently, sometimes even hourly or daily. Therefore, it is important to create levels of hierarchy and visual patterns that ease navigation and access to information.

Because there is a wide range of interfaces, viewing distances, and body positions from which users may access an interface, coming up with a single methodology would be very difficult. The sections below outline ways to approach hierarchy successfully, geared to the most used devices.

Hierarchy in Interfaces

The visual hierarchy of an interface is based on the amount of content in an interface and highlights this content in priority order. For example, a newspaper interface will probably take up a lot of space and be divided into many sections. Concentrate on finding the most important articles and advertisements, and then place the other levels after those. Hierarchy can be effectively created by spacing, leading, font size, and image locations, with all content arranged in the grid created for the interface. By contrast, an interface for a website promoting a product will probably have very little content, filled mostly with promotional imagery.

The main rule of reading began centuries ago with the first book, the Gutenberg Bible. Gutenberg reinforced the Western method of reading left to right when he created the first major printed book, which could be applied to other ways of reading.

Western Reading

This method is called the Gutenberg diagram. It moves from the left (1) to the bottom right (2), creating an angular line, and returns to the top right (3), and finally proceeding, if the reader chooses, to the bottom left once again at an angle. This rule is essential when considering focal points on a page, and it surely reinforces readability.

Right-to-Left Reading (Hebrew and Arabic)

The Gutenberg diagram can be applied to other ways of reading besides Western languages. Hebrew reading begins from right to left and then down at an angle. Then, the reader returns to the top left and goes down in an angle to the bottom right.

Top-to-Bottom Reading (Chinese)

The Eastern world has an optional way of reading top to bottom. It is important when designing top-to-bottom interfaces to be aware of how to apply the Gutenberg diagram successfully to this type of reading. In this case, the diagram would work by starting at the top left and going down to the bottom, and then returning to the top right and then back to the bottom right.

Gutenberg Diagram (Figure 7.1)

Step 1: Place the layout of the interface.

Step 2: Divide the visible space (top, bottom, left, and right) with which the user or reader will interact directly into four quadrants.

Step 3: Primary focus: The reading starts from top left to bottom right (a line at an angle).

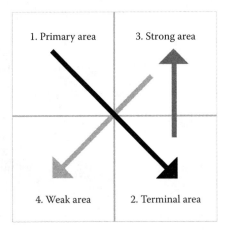

Figure 7.1

Gutenberg diagram.

Step 4: Secondary focus: Returns to the top right.
Step 5: Tertiary focus: Returns at an angle to the bottom left.

Other studies of web design that have become very helpful for designing interfaces include the following.

The F layout is a Visual System (Figure 7.2)

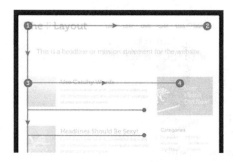

Figure 7.2

F layout system. (Courtesy of Jones, B., 2016, Understanding the F-Layout in Web Design, Web Design Envato Tuts+, http://webdesign.tutsplus.com/articles/ understanding-the-f-layout-in-web-design--webdesign-687.)

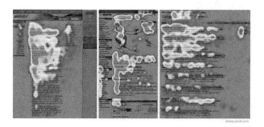

Figure 7.3

Heat maps from user eye-tracking studies of three websites. The areas where users looked the most are colored red; the yellow areas indicate fewer views, followed by the least-viewed blue areas. Gray areas attracted no user fixations. (Courtesy of Nielsen, J., 2016a, F-Shaped Pattern for Reading Web Content, *Jakob Nielsen's Alertbox (blog)*, https://www.nngroup.com/articles/f-shaped-pattern-reading-web-content/.)

According to Jakob Nielsen (2016a), most users end up reading from left to right and then down. This eye-tracking motion happens several times, as needed, according to the amount and length of the information on an interface (Figure 7.3). This F layout can be applied not only to websites but also to app interfaces, operating systems, and so on. According to Nielsen, the *F* stands for *fast*. He recognized in over 232 user tests how users typically move their attention from left to right. This continuous pattern will work only with languages read from left to right. Concerning these eye-tracking studies, most of the content in the examples was located on the left side, including the column of text. Therefore, if the content looks different than the example interface used for the study, users' eye-tracking will vary.

Understanding the Z-Layout

The Z-layout is a very direct system that takes the user's point of view from left to right, then back to a lower point of the screen on the left, and then straight to the right. It is important to take into consideration whether any app or website will fit this method of eye-tracking well or not; the user's eye-tracking should be natural and not forced. Therefore, it is important to do eye-tracking tests to determine the hierarchy that users will see on the page, remembering that first impressions are very important. In Figure 7.4, the Z-layout is aligned consistently with the app behind it.

Scrolling in Hierarchy

Scrolling is part of many interfaces, because often the information to present does not fit on a screen all at once. Hoa Loranger (2016) mentioned that it is important to pay attention to the amount of scrolling we put on websites, a concern, I believe, that also applies to apps or any other type of interface with scrolling content. Consider whether pagination might be better instead. Jakob Nielsen (2016b) used eye-tracking data to help us understand the percentage of viewing time users spend on a page where the length is measured by pixels per page, showing that the longer users scroll, the faster they lose interest. The line on Figure 7.5 represents the "fold," the content that can show on one screen of 800 vertical pixels. This study gives us parameters to keep in mind when designing for screens that are 800 pixels.

Scrolling studies present essential knowledge regarding the limits and boundaries of scrolling for creating interface hierarchy. The designer must keep in mind that more scrolling creates more frustration and willingness to go to another page (Figure 7.6).

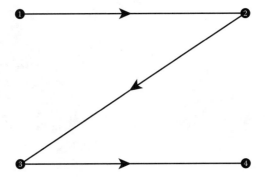

Figure 7.4

Z-layout.

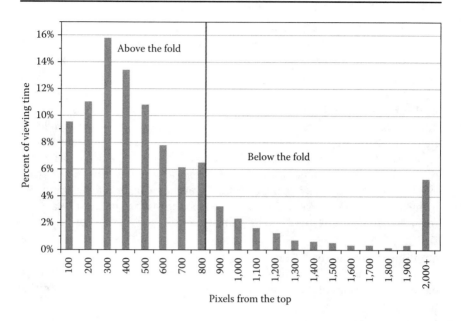

Figure 7.5

Viewing time study.

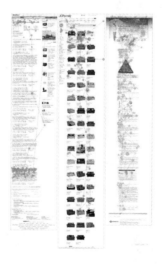

Figure 7.6

Eye-tracking study of scrolling.

7. Visual Hierarchy

Size

Follow guidelines and proportions to effectively create an interface at the correct size.

Scale

Using scale to add hierarchy is essential. Do not just "eyeball it"; do user testing throughout the design process. Study other design patterns that other interfaces have successfully executed. Rather than copying, apply the rules and guidelines they have applied.

Contrast

Contrast is everything in an interface and may include many aspects, such as color, shape, size, scale, and even negative and positive space. Making sure that the interface has a sense of contrast helps balance the content, including the navigation.

Color

As mentioned in Chapter 4, color is essential even if using just black, white, and the grays in between. Rather than just a palette, color is the visual language that represents an entire interface. Poor use of color could cause serious consequences, especially for users who are visually impaired.

Repetition

It is important to repeat patterns in the interface. For example, repeat the location of navigational element so that the user can find them easily. In addition, visual patterns can be made, usually created to brand the interface. These can be placed at lower levels of the hierarchy, in the background of the interface.

Alignment

Alignment is an essential part of the grid, considered in more detail in the following chapter. When objects, images, or text are aligned, it suggests that they belong to the same idea. If they are not aligned, it creates chaos in the interface.

Proximity

Grouping and creating proximity in the content creates levels of hierarchy. For example, the main navigation cannot be spread out all over the interface. All links must have close proximity to create a level of hierarchy. For this reason, the main menu is usually located in the top right or left of the screen, because it has extremely high priority.

Dominance

Most likely, some kind of dominant content will be present—headlines or images that capture attention first.

Emphasis

Emphasis can be created by a focal point in the interface.

Typography

Most likely, the interface will be typographically influenced, because we cannot communicate in text without typography. Therefore, it is important to create a visual hierarchy using the typographic content effectively and in balance with color, image, scale, and contrast. For more information on type, visit Chapter 5 concerning typography, icons, and user legibility.

Design Patterns

Awareness of design patterns began in 1979 with architect Christopher Alexander's book, *The Timeless Way of Building*. The book describes in incredible detail the use of patterns in homes and provides his opinion of these patterns and how users and the space in their homes interact.

Later, at the 1989 Object-Oriented Programming Conference, Ward Cunningham and Kent Beck submitted a presentation of five patterns and their successful use of those patterns for window-based graphical UIs (Beck 1987).

The rules and guidelines for design patterns have been tailored to all types of interfaces. For example, an interface for an Apple smartphone might have completely different design patterns from those for an Android phone. Though both are smartphones, we interact with their hierarchies in extremely different ways. Therefore, avoid general assumptions about how patterns should be created in an interface. There are thousands of patterns and ways to make a successful interface. Rely on user testing, and remember that every interface must follow rules and guidelines given by the human centered guidelines of the operating system of the device.

Eye Gaze Patterns

One of the most important rules to follow is *do not reinvent the wheel*. Don't only follow device guidelines but also use icons and ways of arranging images with which users are familiar. As mentioned above, organize the content by following the user's visual order. Though I do not suggest you copy other layouts, learn from their composition and patterns and devise an idea that will not alienate your users. Sometimes, interfaces can appear so complex that the user will give up before even trying to access the information.

It is also important to look at the design groupings—for example, the links that create the main navigation and how that creates hierarchy within the interface.

Understanding Visual Patterns

The most common visual patterns are discussed below.

Login Patterns

The login pattern is one of the most commonly used in our everyday lives with computer interfaces (Beck et al. 2016), because we have to log in to check our email, visit a social media website or app, or check our bank account online. Our routine daily tasks involve logging into accounts. Consider a login like a door, an entrance to whatever is accessed behind it. Therefore, it is extremely important and most likely used almost everywhere, especially if we want to be part of a community. In addition, the login pattern gives the user a sense of security—not everyone can see all their personal information and it does not waste their time by trying to teach them a new pattern in order to log in. Overall, the process of logging in should be intuitive (Figures 7.7 and 7.8).

Figure 7.7

Login patterns from different social media websites: Facebook, Vimeo, and Dribbble.

Figure 7.8

Login patterns from different banks, from left to right: Capital One, Citibank, and Wells Fargo.

Navigation Pattern

After login, navigation is one of the most essential visual patterns. Users will become familiar with your navigation. If an interface layout changes completely, users can become extremely overwhelmed to the point that they no longer want to use that interface. It is better to introduce changes to an interface little by little. Rather than taking away the creativity of the designer, design patterns that enrich and inspire, because good patterns will help the user and the interface to work better.

Patterns are not always the same between operating systems. For example, the case below considers the very different UI guidelines for iOS and Android regarding the hamburger icon.

Spotify: An App Case Study
(Removing the Hamburger Icon from the Hierarchy)

With a library of over 30 million songs, Spotify is one of the most-downloaded apps in both iOS and Android for listening to music (Windows Central 2015). The hamburger icon became a controversial visual element for Spotify.

The hamburger icon had been previously added to the app's UI, as shown on the smartphone screenshot to the left of Figure 7.9. Spotify did user testing after changing the hamburger menu symbol to tab bar navigation at the bottom, finding that 9% of users interacted more with the app in general and 30% more interacted with the actual tab bar than they did with the hamburger icon (Perez 2016). These tests also revealed, according to the company, that reducing the number of options on the bottom tab bar to five increased the reach of Spotify's programmed content (Figure 7.10). Tests were given to both new and old users, and the user researchers found no negative effects. Instead, they found that the users interacted more with the content of the app itself.

This is a very helpful study for understanding when to use the hamburger icon and when to use a tab bar. Again, the tab bar works very well for Spotify, but it may not work as well for other apps. Regardless, it is worth a try to apply

Figure 7.9

Old version of the Spotify app.

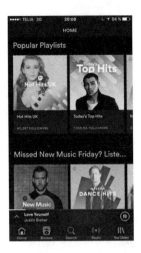

Figure 7.10

New version of the Spotify app, with new tab bar at the bottom.

this example to your project and to the development of the design pattern you are trying to resolve. Though the hamburger icon can be very helpful, it may not be so helpful if it appears in an interface from the beginning, because it creates a sense that you are hiding information from the user, and it takes the user some time to even get around to the icon. Analyzing this study, it might be important to apply the hamburger icon only in second- or even third-level navigation, because it is possible that users tend to avoid hamburger navigation unless they really need it.

This case shows how hierarchy can change a company's revenue and enable users to access more of their content. Visual hierarchy is an evolving process in the UI design world, because content and software are always changing and because users always want improvement and innovation. Improving visual hierarchy is, therefore, a constant, never-ending effort for a competitive UI.

GoDaddy Case Study

GoDaddy (http://www.godaddy.com) is one of the most sought-after domain and hosting servicing providers, serving Internet clients, developers, and DIY users trying to build their own websites. The evolution of this website from 2006 to 2016 in terms of hierarchy was quite dramatic, as shown below (Figures 7.11 through 7.13).

In 2006 (WiredPrairie.us 2016), the UI of the GoDaddy website was very crowded and overwhelming, with a lot of information. The contrast and the content were not clear. At that time, this website used only default fonts.

By 2011 (Allemann 2013), the hierarchy of the website showed more contrast between the navigation and the dominant element on the page, the photo in the middle of the right side page. It is important to mention that faces and enlarged

Figure 7.11

Older GoDaddy interface from 2006.

Figure 7.12

Older GoDaddy interface from 2013.

Figure 7.13

Older GoDaddy interface from 2013.

7. Visual Hierarchy

people—especially faces—grab more of our attention than anything else, as testing of our visual perception has shown (Davies and Hoffman 2002). In addition, this website still used browsers' default fonts.

The 2016 version of the website (GoDaddy 2016) shows a clear hierarchy and contrast between navigation, branding, and content. It is very user-friendly and easy on the eyes. In addition, the website now uses a custom font, rather than browsers' default web fonts, which reinforces the website's branding.

External Sources for Pattern Libraries

Below is a wide range of pattern libraries.

1. UI Patterns: http://ui-patterns.com/patterns
2. Elements of Design: http://www.smileycat.com/design_elements/
3. CSSbake Ingredients: http://www.cssbake.com/ingredients/
4. Pattern Browser: http://www.patternbrowser.org/code/pattern/pattern. php?4,1,1,1,8
5. Public Patterns: http://quince.infragistics.com/html/AllPatterns.aspx
6. Patternry: http://patternry.com/patterns/
7. Mobile UI Patterns: http://www.mobile-patterns.com/
8. Inspired UI: http://inspired-ui.com/
9. Yahoo! Design Pattern Library: https://developer.yahoo.com/ypatterns/
10. Welie.com Pattern Library: http://www.welie.com/patterns/index.php
11. Pattern Tap: http://patterntap.com/tags/types

References

Allemann, Andrew. 2013. GoDaddy Says It's Go Time: New Marketing, Improved Site – Domain Name Wire | Domain Name News & Views. *Domain Name Wire | Domain Name News & Views.* Accessed April 21, 2017. http://domainnamewire. com/2013/09/05/godaddy-says-its-go-time-new-marketing-improved-site/.

Beck, Kent, Temre N., and Cunningham, W. 1987. *Using Pattern Languages for Object-Oriented Programs.* Accessed July 28, 2016. http://c2.com/doc/ oopsla87.html.

Davies, Temre N., and Donald D. Hoffman. 2002. Attention to Faces: A Change-Blindness Study. *Perception* 31(9): 1123–46.

GoDaddy. 2016. Domain Names | The World's Largest Domain Name Registrar—GoDaddy. *GoDaddy.* Accessed April 21, 2017. https://www.godaddy.com.

Jones, Brandon. 2016. Understanding the F-Layout in Web Design. *Web Design Envato Tuts+.* Accessed April 21, 2017. http://webdesign.tutsplus.com/ articles/understanding-the-f-layout-in-web-design--webdesign-687.

Loranger, Hoa. 2016. *Infinite Scrolling Is Not for Every Website.* Accessed April 21, 2017. https://www.nngroup.com/articles/infinite-scrolling/.

Nielsen, Jakob. 2016a. F-Shaped Pattern for Reading Web Content. *Jakob Nielsen's Alertbox (blog).* Accessed April 21, 2017. https://www.nngroup. com/articles/f-shaped-pattern-reading-web-content/.

Nielsen, Jakob. 2016b. Scrolling and Attention. *Jakob Nielsen's Alertbox (blog)*. Accessed April 21, 2017. https://www.nngroup.com/articles/scrolling-and-attention/.

Perez, Sarah. 2016. Spotify Ditches the Controversial "Hamburger" Menu in iOS App Redesign. *TechCrunch*. Accessed April 21, 2017. http://social.techcrunch.com/2016/05/03/spotify-ditches-the-controversial-hamburger-menu-in-ios-app-redesign/.

Windows Central. 2015. Spotify for Windows Phone Updated with an iOS-Esque Visual Revamp. *Windows Central*. Accessed April 21, 2017. http://www.windowscentral.com/spotify-updates-windows-phone-app-ios-esque-visual-revamp.

WiredPrairie.us. 2016. Too many links at GoDaddy? Accessed April 21, 2017. https://www.wiredprairie.us/journal/2006/01/.

8

Grid Flexibility and Responsiveness

The Grid

Grids are structures that are created for websites, apps, or other types of software systems. Although they are most likely invisible to the eye, without a grid the content could become extremely disorganized. One thing all grids have in common is the need to be updated constantly because of technological advancements. Some grids need to be flexible, capable of responding to different screen sizes, while others must be more static, because of the nature of the targeted hardware and software, such as an ATM machine.

Other Examples

A grid is like a bookshelf with dividers that allow you to organize your books by order or preferred categories. Without a bookshelf, all the books would be disorganized, probably in a heap on the floor. A grid is also like our bones, without which we would not be able to stand or keep our organs located in the right places. The grid in a UI is just as important as the structure of our skeletons.

Beginning

When you begin to create a grid, spending time sketching will save you time in the long run, especially if you already have content with which to work provided by the client. Without real content, it will be hard to set the grid metrically because you will not know how many paragraphs are needed or what list is needed for the navigation. Do not rush when you are creating a grid. Only start once you have all the information necessary; if you try to rush, you will spend twice the time because you are working without the entire content.

Our whole world involves grids. Buildings, containers, and streets are all designed using a grid, as are even our clothes and shoes. Without grids, our world would not be organized.

A grid not only serves an organizational purpose but also helps us work faster, because once we have a set grid, we can easily organize content according to the guidelines proposed. It is important to be in agreement with the developer in order to ascertain whether your plans are practical and achievable. Testing sessions with various types of grids are recommended.

Modular Grid

A modular grid is a well-known type of grid frequently used by print designers. It is also used in UI design, because we handle content very similarly, and our goal is to help the user or reader to access the information clearly.

Parts of a modular grid (Figure 8.1):

1. *Columns* consist of vertical guides that enable the creation of columns of text of different thickness ranges. They also help us align the text and images vertically.
2. *Flowlines* are horizontal guides that help us control the alignment horizontally.
3. *Margins* are the negative area that surrounds the information. Margins are usually optional and most likely are not used because the content usually takes over the entire space.
4. *Spatial zones* are modules that can be filled by grouping. This means grouping vertical and horizontal areas to create a larger area of hierarchy.
5. *Markers* are used where logos, main navigation, or any type of information is placed all the time in most interfaces.
6. *Modules* are units that are created by the intersection of the vertical and horizontal lines that create the guides.

The Value of Pixels

For UIs, the grid is extremely strict because every pixel counts. It is important to know how many pixels are added by icons or paragraphs. Do not use inches or points, measurements that are for print media, even for typefaces. Resolution is also important, because of older devices such as the first iPhone, which was 320×480 pixels, a number that the iPhone 6 more than doubled to 750×1334 pixels. The same effect has happened to many computer screens and other smartphones and tablets made by different companies. Because of the competitive need among companies to provide users with the best resolution, pixels are very important.

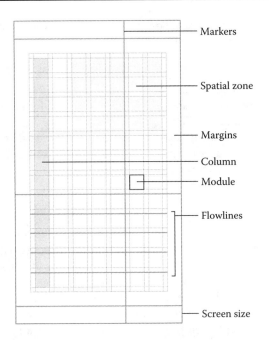

Markers

Spatial zone

Margins

Column

Module

Flowlines

Screen size

Figure 8.1

Parts of a grid used for a 1280 × 720 screen (Android Tablet). (Courtesy of Müller-Brockmann, J., *Grid Systems in Graphic Design: A Visual Communication Manual for Graphic Designers, Typographers, and Three Dimensional Designers*. Hastings House Pub, 1981.)

When creating a paper prototype, use a pixel ruler to achieve the most accurate understanding of how the layout will be organized. The pixel ruler will not only help you to achieve a digital prototype but will also give you a better idea of the actual size of the interface.

The above example of a prototyping tool called *Justinmind* shows how the ruler option allows you to drag guides and thus helps to place content. Most prototyping tools let you know numerically how many pixels you are using horizontally and vertically to set information in the intended locations.

Keeping Up with Pixels

When creating a grid, make sure you track all the numbers, especially during the beginning of the paper prototyping stage, because when it comes to designing for a similar device, it will make it a lot easier to adjust the grid. In order to control the grid so meticulously, it is necessary to know the specific size of the screen, icon limitations, and what is realistically achievable. Consider the example below.

Following Guidelines

The guidelines of every operating system vary, from the accurate use of icons to the limitations of navigation sizes, including color and contrast. All guidelines have become more flexible over time. I hope they continue to evolve in that direction so that designers can be more creative with space.

Questions to Ask before You Start Making Decisions on a Grid

How much content do I have?

Into how many sections should I divide the content for navigation?

What kind of content is it?

How should I display the content in order to enhance user accessibility?

Do I have more images than text? Is this helpful? Is there enough memory space to achieve short loading time?

Do I have a purely textual project?

How important is the text in the content? Does it provide us with instructions or is it more descriptive?

How important in the hierarchy are the images in the content?

How important in the hierarchy is it for the text to stand out?

On what kind of device will the grid be viewed or read?

Make sure to create the grid using a section of the screen that has the most content in order to divide the work area properly. If you start with a screen page that has limited content, then you will have to start over again, because the grid you designed for the least amount of content will not fit a screen page with a lot of content. Therefore, by working first with a screen page with more content and then finding a balance and bridging the gap between it and the one with the least content, you will achieve a strong, flexible grid.

There is so much history on grids that a thorough study would require a book of its own. So, in this chapter, we describe the grids that are the most common. From there, you can be creative and come up with your own grid that fits the content with which you are working.

Types of Grids

As a first step to making grids, start with a column. If you think you need more structure, you can add two columns, then three columns, and maybe even four columns. It all depends on the size limitations you have.

When working with the content, you need to find the focal point so that when the user enters the UI, he or she can easily distinguish the hierarchy (Figure 8.2).

There are a few rules to take into consideration—the rule of thirds and the phi diagram are very similar and they help us create a dynamic structure within the space. It needs to guide the eye of the user, indicating where he or she should look and in what order. These rules are most helpful for interfaces that are primarily image oriented.

The rule was originally created in the context of photography, book design, and the visual arts in general, but now interface design implements this method in grid creation—sometimes because visual UI grids are interactive, constantly changing, and updating due to technology. It is important that we consider all the content, including navigation, windows, tabs, and galleries.

8. Grid Flexibility and Responsiveness

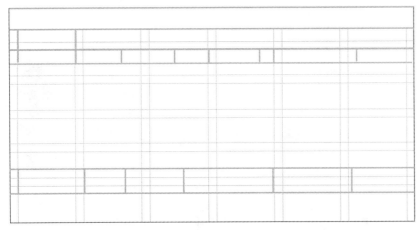
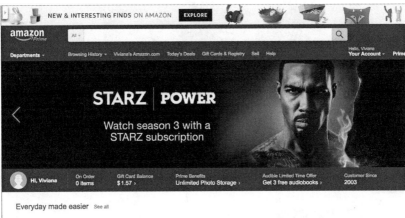

Figure 8.2

Amazon website showing the focal point in the center of the homepage.

It does not matter how many differently sized devices or projections the app or website needs to have. What matters is that the user not become overwhelmed by drastic changes from one screen to the next. In addition, it is important not to have drastic changes from a vertical to a horizontal layout if the design is responsive both vertically and horizontally. It is not necessary to create a responsive layout if the app's purpose will not allow responsiveness. For example, a game with layouts that are all in landscape will not work vertically aesthetically, and therefore, it would be best to stick with a horizontal layout (Figures 8.3 and 8.4).

Do not force your designs to be responsive or to fit every screen. If it does not fit properly, then you need to analyze closely what went wrong, go back to sketching, and rethink the structure. Moreover, during this stage, it is extremely important to ask for feedback, whether you are sketching on paper or making paper or digital prototypes.

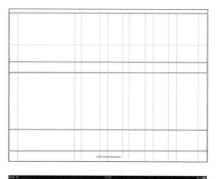

Figure 8.3

Muji to Go app for iPad provides a strong grid structure and branding in the design.

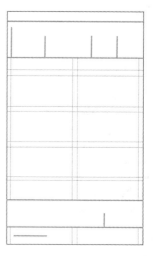

Figure 8.4

HEMA app is well organized and simple to navigate and access.

8. Grid Flexibility and Responsiveness

Limitations

UIs can be extremely creative and user-friendly. One of the most important rules of thumb when starting a UI project is to know how much time you realistically have available to work on the project. In addition, talk to the developer to see how much can be done in that amount of time.

Sometimes, a UI will be unrealistically designed in terms of the amount of time it requires for development before it can be made available to the user, because of the number of developers in a company and their schedules. It is necessary to plan right from the beginning and be aware of the expectations of the designer(s) or developer(s).

Technological Tools

Templates

Many websites use assembled grids and an established structure. As designers, we can easily download and install these in our server space to quickly populate content, including branding, text, images, and navigation.

Content management systems (CMSs) are increasing in popularity by the minute because we need to update our content and keep up with new versions. Using a CMS simplifies these concerns, because only the CMS needs to be updated, and the hosting company of the website is usually in charge of this service.

WordPress software is a world leader in open-source publishing that publishes over 26% of the content on the web, totaling billions of pages. This type of software helps everyone to build their website in a responsive manner, which means that it will work on mobile devices and desktops. WordPress understands the need for a grid that is why it offers many types of themed layouts to suit a variety of interests.

Another open-source software project is Siberian, which helps developers to build apps and provides a wide range of customizable layout options.

Many types of software are out there that can sometimes help to create grids rapidly and, thus, build the final interface. All these types of software help us to get closer as designers to achieving our main goal, which is to build a strong and user-friendly grid with intuitive design patterns. Therefore, it is important for UI designers to stay up to date in regards to these types of technologies to learn their limitations or options. Moreover, templates can be very flexible. The developer needs to understand their limits and let the designer know what is possible and what is not.

Designer and Developer

The relationship between the designer and developer should be very open and flexible. In particular, without compromise between them, it is hard to even decide on the structure of the interface. Therefore, communication is key to sustaining the process of developing the interface from beginning to end.

Sometimes, Templates Are Not an Option

If the designer wants something that cannot be found in a template, then it is important to sketch it out and ask the developer to start from scratch and see whether it is possible. Usually, creating something from scratch takes longer and will incur higher costs.

Responsiveness

Responsiveness is not a necessary part of UI design and is only required if the user needs flexibility and if the designer can make a decision on whether to make it responsive. Usually, it is easier to make a thinner UI responsive to a wider view, compared with making a wider UI responsive to a thinner view.

The need for responsiveness arose when smartphones, tablets, and wearables became popular and mainstream because of the larger number of people using these devices. It is likely that websites and apps are now responsiveness-friendly. Only when the designer and the user decide it is not worth forcing a UI to fit both screens will that UI not be responsive, which can happen and is not bad. For example, if user testing of a game reveals a preference for the horizontal version, then there is no need to make the UI responsive.

Overall, the need for responsiveness will most likely occur when users wish to retrieve, access, or read information when in constant motion, usually walking, running, or standing, or when they are sitting for a few minutes. Therefore, responsiveness is necessary in some cases.

For example, if you are going to retrieve money from an ATM, then you are not going to expect the ATM machine's interface to become responsive because the UI was designed solely for one screen.

Tools for Responsiveness

There are many UI libraries for developers that help with responsiveness. When designing for responsiveness, keep it as close as possible to the main interface. It is usually best to start designing with the smallest version and then move toward the larger version. In that way, you will know the limitations and pressures on the interface design (Figure 8.5).

There are different levels of responsiveness.

1. One device, for example, iOS
2. When two devices need responsiveness, for example, two smartphones, such as iOS and Android
3. When three devices need responsiveness, for example, an Apple phone, Android phone, and Android tablet
4. Apple phone, Apple tablet, Android phone, and Android tablet
5. Apple phone, Apple tablet, Android phone, Android tablet, and Windows phone
6. Apple phone, Apple tablet, Android phone, Android tablet, Windows phone, and Windows tablet
7. And so on

Figure 8.5

Airbnb.com is responsive to various sizes of screens, from desktop to mobile.

Every OS is unique and will have its own limitations and guidelines, starting from the size of its screen. The designer needs to be on top of all these changes, because they can be extremely different from device to device, and so working with the developer is important.

For example, when sketching a grid for iPhone and Android smartphones, there is a need to sketch slightly different grids because they are of different sizes and resolutions. It is similar to going shopping for clothes. Imagine you are going with a friend who is the same age as you but taller. Both of you may get the same type of t-shirt, but you will need to get different sizes. Designing grids for two similar devices that have the same purpose is similar.

User Testing

It is necessary to keep responsiveness in check by using tools such as online testing or paper prototyping. Any kind of user testing applied at any stage is part of the process. For more information about user testing, see Chapters 2 and 13.

References

Curtis, Barry. 2009. The grid book. *Journal of Design History* 22(3): 293–94.

Elam, Kimberly. 2004. *Grid Systems: Principles of Organizing Type*. Princeton Architectural Press, New York.

Greve, Thomas and Greve, Thomas. 2016. Market Design in the Smart Grid. In: *Smart Grid Handbook*, pp. 1–9, Hoboken, NJ.

Higgins, Hannah. 2009. *The Grid Book*. MIT Press, Cambridge, MA.

Hollis, Richard. 2006. *Swiss Graphic Design: The Origins and Growth of an International Style, 1920–1965*. Yale University Press, New Haven, CT.

Hurlburt, Allen. 1982. *Grid: A Modular System for the Design and Production of Newspapers, Magazines, and Books*. Wiley, Hoboken, NJ.

Meggs, Philip B. and Alston W. Purvis. 2016. *Meggs' History of Graphic Design*. Wiley, Hoboken, NJ.

Müller-Brockmann, Josef. 1981. *Grid Systems in Graphic Design: A Visual Communication Manual for Graphic Designers, Typographers, and Three Dimensional Designers*. Braun Publishing, Salenstein, Switzerland.

Roberts, Lucienne, and Julia Thrift. 2005. *The Designer and the Grid*. Rotovision, Brighton Bnq 2RA, UK.

Samara, Timothy. 2005. *Making and Breaking the Grid: A Graphic Design Layout Workshop*. Rockport Publishers, Beverly, MA.

9

Motion

Imagine you are in a classroom. Everyone is seated and quiet, when suddenly someone gets up and leaves the room. What happens? Everybody is going to turn to look at the person in motion. This drastic change in the atmosphere grabs the visual perception of everyone else in the classroom. Motion is a very distinctive way of creating hierarchy because it not only highlights through movement but also through form, color, and even sound. This is why motion pictures are popular, because they serve to entertain the viewer. Though interfaces do not interact with users in completely the same manner, motion in parts of the interface is needed to interact and communicate with the user. The innovation and fluidity of motion should become part of interfaces by creating a balance between the content and the design. Over half the interface includes some type of moving response to interaction, whether opening a window, launching a program by tapping an icon, or even when swiping through windows or pages.

It is important to think about how to make transitions from one page to the next or to a menu simple and transparent. Motion is the interactivity and body language of an interface. There are many types of motion you might brainstorm during the paper prototyping process, and so it is important to ask the developers whether it is possible to create the motion you want to create.

Tips

Motions or animations should not be overwhelming. They should neither take all the attention from the menu nor serve as a distraction. During user testing, whether with paper prototyping or digitally, if a user has found the transition to be distracting, then it will be necessary to find smaller and shorter transitions or maybe even to remove them completely. We do not need motion everywhere on the interface, but only when there is a design decision to add it and when the motion fits the content. A glamorous homepage might be positively received the first time, but if it takes too long to load, then it can become tedious when the viewer uses the interface on a daily basis or several times a day. It is important to prevent the user from becoming bored or fed up with the motions, but at the same time we want users to engage with them every time they use the interface. As such, motions need to be settled, balancing the visual design of the interface. The purpose of motion is to make the interface more accessible, not exhausting.

Motions such as enlarging or resizing when opening a new page or going onto a new screen might be too much. A transition should be shown because it is used as a way to move on to the next step or as an indicator that something has happened. For example, when we click a link, we expect it to change color or do something to indicate that a process has been started. Otherwise, there is the risk that the person clicking might think the link is broken and just a static piece of text, leading to confusion. As such, a slight change such as underlining, color change, bolder font, or transparency is important to add after an active click.

Making Decisions

Small changes can lead to an award-winning interface, but this doesn't mean that you should overdo it. Just because you have found a cool motion that could be applied does not mean that it will be useful or fit the purpose of the interface. Do not look for splashy or cool-looking animations that end up draining the interface. In addition, try to test the motions you have found on users to see whether they enjoy them. Repeated testing is a good idea, as this will help you to observe patterns of behavior rather than just initial reactions. Then, make a final decision about whether or not to apply the motion in the final interface.

Overall, transitions should be extremely short and vary according to their functions. Instead of being dominant, they should become extremely intuitive to the user.

Full Motion Prototype

Many UI designers take the option to create fully animated prototypes using animation software like After Effects. This does not suit all prototypes but may be valuable on a case-by-case basis. It may be needed to show a new type of motion for a new interface that cannot be created in current prototyping tools like XD from Adobe, InVision, or Axure. Fully animated prototypes are great to show the fully working UI without development and understanding of the vision. The only limitation is that no users can interact with the prototype, because it is a video (allowing only one-way interaction, playing the videos until their end). In addition, this is a great way to enable the developers to see the interactive transitions of the application or website in a more realistic way, while also helping users provide feedback on needed changes, even if the prototype can only be tested passively. The full-motion video prototype is a low-cost prototype that helps the user just as much as other types of prototyping. Figure 9.1 shows an example of

Figure 9.1

Titan browser prototype, designed and animated by Nitin Sampathi and Matt Taylor and created in After Effects.

a digital prototype made in After Effects of a browser called Titan. It shows the dynamism and simplicity of how to work with the search bar and have more space to see the content. Also note how the icons are very settled and easy to access, even the hamburger bar on the right.

Preloader (Figure 9.2)

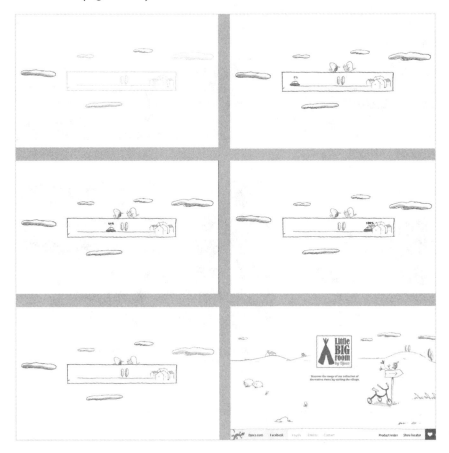

Figure 9.2

Animation used as a preloader for the website Little Big Room by Djeco. (Courtesy of Merci-Michel®, 2016, http://www.little-big-room.com/.)

Transition (Figure 9.3)

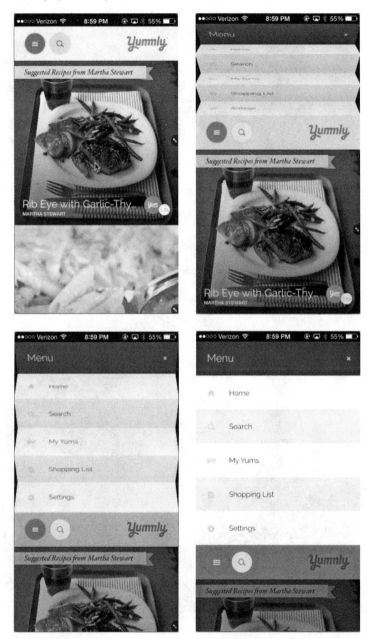

Figure 9.3

Transition in the navigation menu of the Yummly app. (Courtesy of Yummly, Inc., Redwood City, CA, USA, 2016, https://itunes.apple.com/us/app/yummly-recipes-recipe-box/id589625334?mt=8.)

Interface Interstitials (Figures 9.4 and 9.5)

Figure 9.4

Ad for the game Saving Yello running in another app.

Figure 9.5

McDonald's ad on a smartphone.

Ad Guidelines (Figure 9.6)

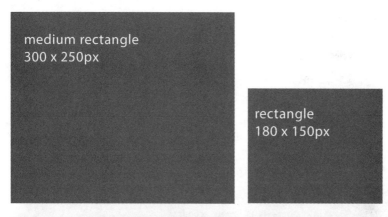
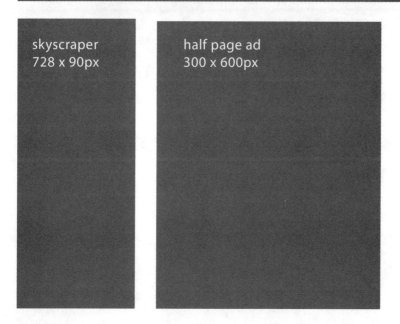

Figure 9.6

Standard ad sizes.

YouTube Ad Examples (Figure 9.7)

youtube.com ad examples

Skippable video ads

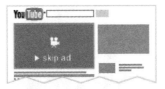

Full video screen, skips after 5 seconds
Desktop, mobile devices, TV, and game
consoles

Non-skippable video ads

Full video screen does not skip maximum
30 seconds
Desktop, mobile devices, TV, and game
consoles

Display ads

Located at the right side of the video
300 × 250 or 300 × 60
Desktop only

Overlay ads

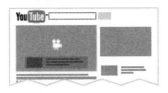

Overlay ad and it appears in the 20% of
the bottom of the video.
468 × 60 or 728 × 90
Desktop only

Sponsored cards

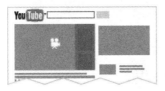

Card sizes vary and they are shown
during the video. They are usually products
related to the video. They only last
few seconds
Desktop and mobile devices

Figure 9.7

Youtube.com is one of the most-used ad supporters online. In 2016, the digital video/motion ad industry climbed from $4.14 billion to $8.04 billion. (Courtesy of Yummly, Inc., Redwood City, CA, USA, 2016, https://itunes.apple.com/us/app/yummly-recipes-recipe-box/id589625334?mt=8.)

Video Interface (Figures 9.8 and 9.9)

Figure 9.8

Video quality that is controllable.

Figure 9.9

Video quality that is fully controllable through motion in the interface.

Windows, Tabs, and Menus (Figure 9.10)

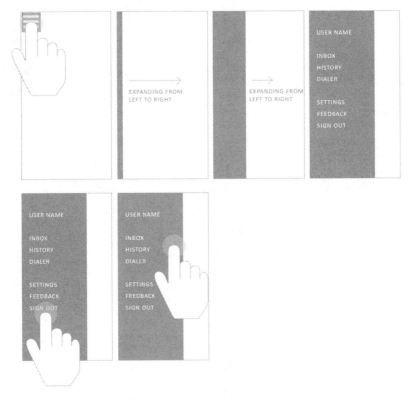

Figure 9.10

The navigation motion moves from left to right when the user interacts with it (this option might change with the writing system if it moves from right to left.)

Gestures and Motions

The gesture technology for interfaces has improved and will soon supersede the mouse and keyboard. In this new era, we will not need to use touch; instead we will use gestures and motions to interact with interfaces. Regardless of this, we still need to design kinetic interfaces that encourage interaction using our whole bodies. In addition to the visual design, it is becoming important to consider how our entire bodies react to an interface, not just our eyes (Figures 9.11 through 9.15). There are very helpful books on gestural interfaces that will guide you to explore this field in more depth, such as Sean Buckley's (engadget 2016).

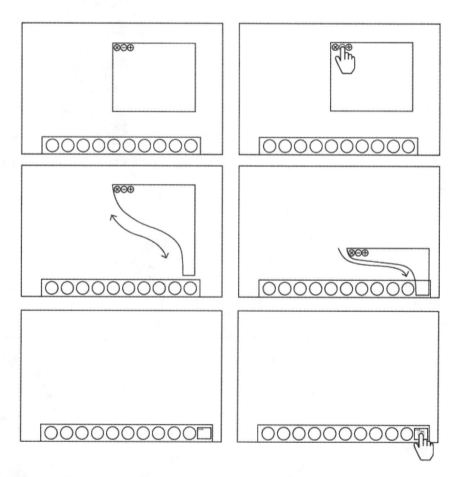

Figure 9.11

Minimize and maximize windows.

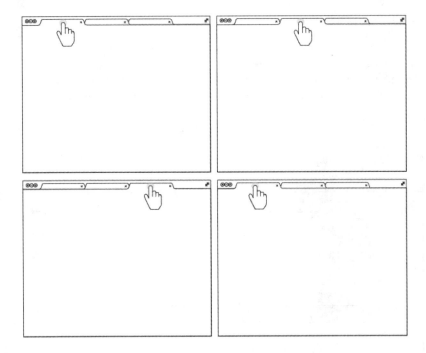

Figure 9.12

Folder tab movement within a browser.

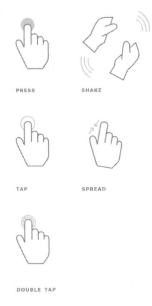

PRESS   SHAKE

TAP   SPREAD

DOUBLE TAP

Figure 9.13

Basic gestures to interact with interfaces.

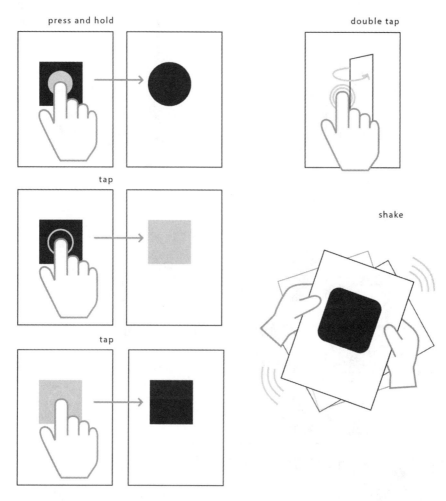

Figure 9.14

Basic gestures to activate motion.

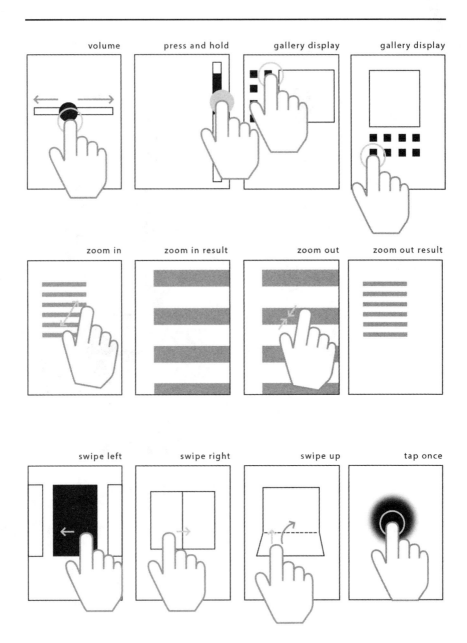

Figure 9.15

Gestures to activate motion.

Types of Menus (Figure 9.16)

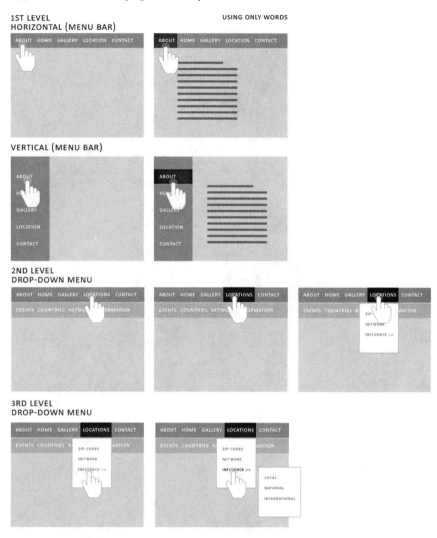

Figure 9.16

Menu types: horizontal, vertical, and drop-down.

Signature Animation and Interactions

This type of animation and interaction in interfaces is the most unique of its kind, and this is why it can call the user's attention faster than another animation or interaction that was seen before (Figure 9.17). Animations and interactions are the essential part of the interface; without them we would not be able to interact effectively with interfaces (BerlinVC 2014).

(a)

(b)

Figure 9.17

Signature interactions. (Courtesy of Vimeo, 2016, https://vimeo.com/37642114.)

References

BerlinVC. 2014. Signature Interactions and Animations for Apps. Accessed May 21, 2016. http://www.berlinvc.com/2014/05/21/signature-interactions-and-animations-for-apps/.

Betancourt, Michael. 2013. *The History of Motion Graphics*. Wildside Press, Rockville, MD.

CMO. 2016. 15 Mind-Blowing Stats About Online Video Advertising. Accessed August 1, 2016. http://www.cmo.com/features/articles/2013/8/27/video_15_mind_blowing.html.

Curran, Steve. 2000. *Motion Graphics: Graphic Design for Broadcast and Film*. Rockport Publishers, Beverly, MA.

engadget. 2016. The Future of Motion Interfaces: Wave Goodbye to the Mouse. 2016. Accessed July 29, 2016. https://www.engadget.com/2013/11/10/motion-gesture-expand/.

Krasner, Jon. 2013. *Motion Graphic Design: Applied History and Aesthetics*. Focal Press, Burlington, MA.

Krasner, Jon, and Jon, Krasner. 2008. Motion Graphics in Interactive Media. In: *Motion Graphic Design*, pp. 68–101.

Merci-Michel®. 2016. Little Big Room by Djeco. Accessed August 1, 2016. http://www.little-big-room.com/.

Motionographer. 2016. Motionographer. Accessed July 29, 2016. http://motionographer.com/.

Vimeo. 2016. Signature Interactions. Accessed August 1, 2016. https://vimeo.com/37642114.

Yummly, Inc. 2016. Yummly Recipes & Recipe Box on the App Store. *App Store*. Accessed August 1, 2016. https://itunes.apple.com/us/app/yummly-recipes-recipe-box/id589625334?mt=8.

SECTION III
Interaction

10

Communication Feedback

This chapter concerns how to test an interface to improve the user's visual awareness of and productivity with the interface.

Feedback on visual communication is an essential and valuable part of the visual interface-design process (Azarask.in, 2016a and 2016b). When asking for feedback during testing, do not be satisfied with simple answers like "it looks good!" or "it looks cool!" You need specific, detailed feedback to make changes and become aware of which specific parts are working effectively, from navigation to type-size legibility and much more.

Whom to Ask?

1. Make sure the people you ask for feedback have the time, willingness, and interest to provide it.
2. Ask people who you are certain will use the interface.
3. Make sure to have at least 30 minutes of their time.
4. Do not pressure the user. Remember, they have not yet had the opportunity to interact with the interface.

How to Ask?

1. Make sure to ask small, direct questions that the user can understand and execute immediately.
2. Plan ahead; test the interface with a colleague before you jump into asking for real user feedback.
3. Be prepared for the amount of time and number of questions you will need to ask.

What to Ask?

1. Introduce your expectations for the users at the beginning.
2. If this is your first testing session, make sure type and symbols are properly legible.
3. Ask about wayfinding and navigation.
4. What is the user's psychological response when interacting with the colors and images?
5. If the examples above are successful, you can start asking more in-depth questions, such as those concerning security and other issues you are trying to resolve.
6. Limit the number of questions you ask. You do not want to overwhelm the user.

Communication

There are three ways to receive feedback. The first, verbal, allows the user and the tester to interact and exchange ideas about the interface being tested. Second, written feedback can be very helpful if a user wants to explain the changes needed in further detail and depth. Lastly, nonverbal communication can reinforce or contradict verbal responses, which can help prompt more testing. According to Dr. Albert Mehrabian (1972), 7% of information is conveyed through words, 38% of information is conveyed through vocal elements, and 55% is conveyed through nonverbal elements, including gestures, body movement, and facial expressions. In contrast, a recent study by Blake Eastman (2016) found that nonverbal communication varies daily from 60% to 90%, depending on the situation and the individual.

When assessing interviews, it is important to take notes about not only verbal feedback but also body language, especially that regarding the interaction between the user and the interface. A user might say the interface works well and explain it in detail, taking a very accommodating attitude, while at the same time plainly struggling to read the navigation and content because the typeface is too small. The user's behavior may reveal struggle through nonverbal communication.

User Behavior

1. Ask the user to speak out loud as they explore the interface so you can hear and receive their feedback.
2. Record the interview by audio or video.

Consider, too, the setting of the interview. Make sure the user feels comfortable. It is advisable to have two people doing the interview to avoid missing details and misunderstandings.

Types of Feedback

Do not let a designer's introverted personality interfere with the receipt of needed feedback. In addition, any misunderstandings regarding the goals of the interface should be clarified from the beginning of the project.

Your work is not an unchangeable work of art. Avoid attachment to it. Stay flexible and open to feedback, options, and changes. Many designers become so attached to their work that they do not want to change it at all, but the design is meant for the users, not as a design itself.

Feedback may be received throughout the different project stages. Even once available to the public, any active interface will need to continue a process of reinvention, because technology is constantly evolving. This need is particularly acute for social media apps, educational software, and merchant websites. Whether the interface is simple or complex, it will still need periodic redesign to fix bugs and implement user requests. For example, Sergey Brin and Larry Page created the first interface for the Google site in January 1996 as a research project. The first Google web page (Figure 10.1) had inconsistent colors between the brand identity and the navigation or body of the website. This relationship has been constantly evolving over time, with Google in 2015 (Figure 10.2) creating its own identity typeface called *Product Sans* (Figure 10.3).

The Google identity is extremely unique, not only in the color system but also with its simple, modern layout defined by the search bar in the center. That element has not changed since its creation, and there is also continuity between the versions of the logo. Google's identity typeface gives users a new sense of security and recognition while they use Google products (Swanner 2015).

Figure 10.1

Branding of the Google website in 1998.

Figure 10.2

Branding of the Google website in 2015.

Figure 10.3

Product Sans typéface. (Courtesy of Google, https://storage.googleapis.com/g-design/static/product-sans-specimen.pdf.)

Interface Preference Settings

It is increasingly important to provide interface options, including for background, typeface size, icon size, and color-blindness awareness. Many of these options are often considered as extra, but with interfaces reaching an ever-more global market, the needs of different users must be considered. Many users will decide not to buy a product if it lacks certain options, because it will not be accessible to them. Therefore, as a designer, remember to place these types of options in the interface. For example, around 10% of men worldwide are color-blind; that extra 10% can only be reached by an interface with this option. For more information about accessibility, see Chapter 12. For information on color blindness, see Chapter 4.

Design Team Feedback

Feedback from your design team about an interface will generally only concern aesthetics, because they have seen its progress from sketches to digital form. Receiving such feedback constantly is essential when working aesthetically.

Part of the manifesto of ZURB (ZURB, Inc. 2016) is to ask "why?" five times when giving feedback to reach the root of a problem. They found that doing so resolves problems more deeply and faster. Rather than leaving unresolved problems, it is better to resolve them at the beginning. Otherwise, a problem will come back later and take longer to resolve, with a bigger structure already on top of the root problem.

Client Feedback

As the client provides the funding, the designer needs to make sure that the client agrees with the way the interface has turned out. Allow the client to sketch their own ideas if they want to make changes. Usually, clients do not know how to sketch properly, so be patient and introduce them to the sketching process so that they feel comfortable explaining their ideas. Sketching is not only for designers. It can be very helpful for clients to sketch to resolve their ideas and thinking. The designer, however, must help them realize their vision, in which regard looking from the big picture to the small details is essential. In addition, keep in mind that clients are always thinking about how the final product of their investment will generate revenue.

User Feedback

Users should be constantly involved in feedback throughout the process. Make sure the users suit the project. You can evaluate them easily by asking a few questions to start. Because the user needs to interact with the interface, if the user is not interested in the interface, the designer will not be able to get good feedback. Be aware that users are usually busy, so keep it very simple and direct. According to Jacob Nielsen, it is optimal to test with five people, after which the answers you get will become repetitive.

Positive Feedback

Positive feedback reinforces what works in the created interface, which is one less thing to change! Keep in mind that one individual saying the menu works very well doesn't mean anything. A majority of users agreeing clearly confirms feedback as true.

Negative Feedback

Negative feedback is usually more important than positive feedback because it helps the designer to resolve problems. The more negative feedback, the fewer problems future users will have when interacting with the interface.

References

Azarask.in. *How To Critique An Interface « Aza on Design*. 2016a. Accessed December 15, 2016. http://www.azarask.in/blog/post/how-to-critique-an-interface/.

Azarask.in. *How To Critique An Interface « Aza on Design*. 2016b. Accessed December 15, 2016. http://www.azarask.in/blog/post/how-to-critique-an-interface/.

Cabrillo Community College District. 2016. *Giving Constructive Feedback*. Accessed December 15, 2016. https://www.cabrillo.edu/services/jobs/pdfs/giving-feedback.pdf.

Eastman, Blake. 2016. How Much of Communication Is Really Nonverbal? *Body Language Classes, Research, and Consulting | Nonverbal Group | NYC*. Accessed December 15, 2016. http://www.nonverbalgroup.com/2011/08/how-much-of-communication-is-really-nonverbal.

Eyal, Nir. 2014. *Hooked: How to Build Habit-Forming Products*. Penguin, City of Westminster, London, UK.

Mehrabian, Albert. 1972. *Nonverbal Communication*. Transaction Publishers, Piscataway, NJ.

Mehrabian, Albert. 1981. *Silent Messages: Implicit Communication of Emotions and Attitudes*. Wadsworth Publishing Company, Belmont, CA.

Mogensen, Christian. 2016. Feedback in User Interface Design | SuperOffice Blog. *CRM Blog: Articles, Tips and Strategies by SuperOffice*. Accessed December 15, 2016. http://www.superoffice.com/blog/feedback/.

Schoedel, Amanda. 2016. 7 Simple Rules for Giving Great Design Feedback | Amanda Schoedel Creative. 2016. *Amanda Schoedel Creative*. Accessed April 24, 2017. http://amandaschoedel.com/blog/give-great-design-feedback/.

Swanner, Nate. 2015. Google Created an Entirely New Typeface (Product Sans) for Its Snappy Logo Redesign. *The Next Web*. Accessed April 21, 2017. http://thenextweb.com/google/2015/09/01/google-created-an-entirely-new-typeface-for-its-snappy-logo-redesign/.

Tognazzini, Bruce. 2014. First Principles of Interaction Design (Revised & Expanded). *askTog*. Accessed April 24, 2017. http://asktog.com/atc/principles-of-interaction-design/.

Toxboe, Anders. 2016. *Feedback Loops Design Pattern*. Accessed December 15, 2016. http://ui-patterns.com/patterns/Feedback-loops.

ZURB, Inc. 2016. *ZURB Manifesto*. Accessed December 10, 2016. http://zurb.com/manifesto.

Accessibility

Making sure your interface reaches a wide range of people with and without disabilities not only expands the number of users as much as possible but also allows users who cannot access more limited interfaces to access your interface. Consider accessibility carefully. Many users may be dissatisfied with interfaces that are too bright, with too-small typefaces, or indistinguishable colors for color-blind people. These are a few examples that people can encounter right away.

An entire field, termed *human-centered design* (Kolko 2015), involves resolving problems focused entirely on human thinking and behavior. This chapter focuses on how our visual experience will affect the user interface and provides options to expand the possible user group.

When creating an interface, have a section in the settings for accessibility options. You can also have accessibility options in the main menu, depending on how important such options are for the particular interface. According to the ISO, accessibility options should be presented before logging in.

Color and Contrast

Regarding color, be aware of some people's limitations in terms of the range of colors they can see. Further explanation of color blindness may be found in Chapter 4.

In addition, visit colorsafe.co for colors that are safe for the web. Following the accessibility guidelines for web interfaces according to the W3C (W3C 2016), small text should have a contrast ratio of at least 4.5:1 against its background and large text (at 14 pt bold/18 pt regular and up) should have a contrast ratio of at least 3:1 (Babich 2016).

Color blindness may be simulated in Adobe Photoshop software.

The interface image in Figure 11.1 is open in Photoshop. From the main menu bar at the top, select View > Proof Setup > Color Blindness—Protanopia-type to convert the image to how a human with protanopia sees it, as shown in Figure 11.2.

Figure 11.1

App interface, puzzle for children. (Courtesy of Hallgren, L., et al., 2016, Puzzle for Children: Kids Game—Android Apps on Google Play, https://play.google.com/store/apps/details?id=com.tappyhappy.puzzleforchildren&hl=en.)

Figure 11.2

App interface, puzzle for children, as it would be viewed by an individual with protanopia in Photoshop. (Courtesy of Hallgren, L., et al., 2016, Puzzle for Children: Kids Game—Android Apps on Google Play, https://play.google.com/store/apps/details?id=com.tappyhappy.puzzleforchildren&hl=en.)

Figure 11.3

App interface, puzzle for children, as it would be viewed by an individual with deuteranopia in Photoshop. (Courtesy of Hallgren, L., et al., 2016, Puzzle for Children: Kids Game—Android Apps on Google Play, https://play.google.com/store/apps/details?id=com.tappyhappy.puzzleforchildren&hl=en.)

Open the interface image in Photoshop. From the main menu bar at the top, select View > Proof Setup > Color Blindness—Deuteranopia-type. The image will change to how a human with deuteranopia sees it, as shown in Figure 11.3.

Inverting Color

The interface should allow inversion of the colors. For example, if the interface has a white background by default, an option to swap to a black background will allow users to access the interface in various environments, from a dark office space to a bright sunny day. Even providing something in between, a gray option, might be advisable. The same holds for interfaces with a colored background. For example, if the default is light blue, a range from light to dark blue will provide options to access the interface in various environments. The main goal is to ensure the user's readability and accessible interaction at all times.

Contrast and Brightness

Interfaces should provide a wide range of options for contrast and brightness. Therefore, make the color palette of the interface consistent and clear throughout.

Screen Magnification

Provide an option in the settings that allows the user to increase the size and minimize the interface. Some users want to see a close-up, detailed version, while others will want to zoom out.

Option to Change Font Size

Giving the user the option to change the font size will help with readability (AndroidPIT 2016). These options can be labeled *small, medium, large,*

---

and *extra-large* or can be expressed as a numerical range of options, such as 10px–25px. The options will vary with the size of the screen and intended location of the user. For example, an app on a tablet will require completely different options than if the interface is projected far from the user.

Text-to-Speech and Speech-to-Text

These tools are very helpful in interfaces with a lot of text or spoken words, respectively, for blind or hard-of-hearing persons. Provide a setting to enable these tools under accessibility.

Icons and Modes for Older Users

If the interface provides a variety of options for the user, make sure all information is clearly organized, especially for hearing impaired and visually impaired users. Mostly it is elderly users who have these impairments, comprising a third of the entire aged population (Lichtenstein 1992). Interfaces meant for this type of user must have a very high volume option, and the system of the interface must be simple, including menus, icons, and overall content, along with options for different sizes.

Visual Feedback

When starting to design an interface, highlight visually, through hierarchy, the interactive links or important parts of the interface for the user when they first arrive (Figure 11.4). This is especially helpful for users who are not used to computer interfaces or when the interface has changed drastically from a previous version. Providing a visual tutorial before enabling navigation will reduce the user's initial confusion, whether that confusion is because they are interacting with the interface for the first time or because the entire visual experience has been rearranged without advance notice.

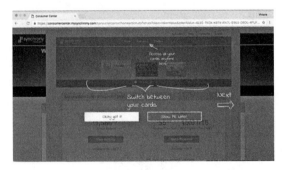

Figure 11.4

Synchrony Bank interface with visual feedback. (Courtesy of Synchrony Financial, 2016, MySynchrony Consumer Financing | Synchrony Bank, https:// www.mysynchrony.com/mysyf/home.html?.)

Forms, Labels, and Boxes

Many new interfaces have taken out the labels for forms, including that information instead inside the form elements themselves (Figure 11.5). When you click or tap, the label disappears, and you can place the information inside. This method actually confuses many users; sometimes they forget what to write in the text box. It is better to provide labels separate from the text input boxes (Figure 11.6).

Figure 11.5

Twitter account website. The Twitter account website, under "Sign Up," provides a form for users to fill out. This form is effective, but having the text inside the text box makes it a bit more complex for some users, who need to remember the label after it disappears. (Courtesy of Twitter, 2016, Sign up, https://twitter.com/signup?lang=en.)

Figure 11.6

Ziggo's account creation webpage, showing separate labels and text boxes. The Ziggo account creation webpage provides a form for users to fill out with labels to the left of the text boxes. Users need not remember the label while filling in each text box. (Courtesy of Ziggo, Utrecht, The Netherlands, 2016, https://www.ziggo.nl/mijn/registreren/stap1/.)

On-Screen Keyboard

Having a keyboard always available is essential when interacting with and designing the interface, even in the early stages of prototyping. If the interface is gestural, an on-screen keyboard is required instead of a physical keyboard. This keyboard should appear automatically after tapping or clicking on a text box.

Autocomplete

When typing in a text box, the interface should guess what the user might want to write, which very helpfully saves the user time and typing (Figure 11.7).

Figure 11.7

The Google search engine provides autocomplete typing. In the case above, the user has entered only "begi" into the search box. Google offers autocomplete options to help the user and makes a search faster if the guess is accurate.

Navigation

There are so many types of hierarchical menus for interfaces, from basic to complex, that it would be impossible to generalize how to implement accessibility for all of them. One main concern is when the user is left-handed. According to Hardyck and Petrinovich (1977), 10% of the population is left-handed. It is important to study, analyze, and resolve accessibility issues for left-handed people, whether they are using a mouse or interacting with a multitouch interface or virtual reality. Many companies are now thinking in depth about how to add some type of setting that rearranges and adapts the interface layout to allow left-handed people to interact with the interface more comfortably and adaptably (Inverse 2016). Since 2014, Android phones have had a feature to rearrange the interface layout for left-handed users (Reid 2016), so many left-handed users are able to use their left thumbs to quickly interact with their Android mobile devices.

Custom Icons and Functions for Impediments

Many more accessibility needs will vary with user needs. Meeting many of these needs will depend on the interface designer to help resolve the problem visually.

There is no "one size fits all." An interface for a specific type of person with several disabilities will be very different compared with mainstream interfaces.

For example, for an icon activating a voice-operation function, the hierarchy of its location will vary with the needs of the user. Another example is the sound function, which is essential for hearing. Being able to control this function through various options is very helpful. Speech recognition is very helpful for someone who cannot type, and text-to-speech, also known as a *screen reader*, helps those who cannot read visually to hear text out loud. To make an interface accessible and fulfill users' needs, designers must test thoroughly and remain aware of the unlimited possibilities of certain functions.

References

AndroidPIT. 2016. Android Accessibility Settings: 5 Hidden Options Everyone Should Be Using—AndroidPIT. *AndroidPIT*. Accessed December 15, 2016. https://www.androidpit.com/android-accessibility-settings.

Babich, Nick. 2016. Accessible Interface Design. UX Planet. https://xplanet.org/accessible-interface-design-3c59ee3ec730.

Hallgren, Ludwig, Sten, Malin, and Shah, Girish. 2016. Puzzle for Children: Kids Game—Android Apps on Google Play. Accessed December 15, 2016. https://play.google.com/store/apps/details?id=com.tappyhappy.puzzleforchildren&hl=en.

Hardyck, Curtis, and Lewis F. Petrinovich. 1977. Left-Handedness. *Psychological Bulletin* 84(3): 385–404.

Inverse. 2016. Apple Patents Special Left-Handed iPhone Mode. Inverse. Accessed December 13, 2016. https://www.inverse.com/article/17601-left-handed-iphone-users-rejoice-apple-patents-special-southpaw-mode.

Karlson, Amy K., Benjamin B. Bederson, and Jose L. Contreras-Vidal. n.d. Understanding One-Handed Use of Mobile Devices. In *Handbook of Research on User Interface Design and Evaluation for Mobile Technology*, pp. 86–101, HCI (Proceedings of the Human Computer Interaction), New York.

Kolko, Jon. 2015. *Exposing the Magic of Design: A Practitioner's Guide to the Methods and Theory of Synthesis*. Oxford University Press, New York.

Lichtenstein, M. J. 1992. Hearing and Visual Impairments. *Clinics in Geriatric Medicine* 8(1): 173–82.

Parhi, Pekka, Amy K. Karlson, and Benjamin B. Bederson. 2006. Target Size Study for One-Handed Thumb Use on Small Touchscreen Devices. In *Proceedings of the 8th Conference on Human-Computer Interaction with Mobile Devices and Services—MobileHCI '06*. doi:10.1145/1152215.1152260, IGI Global, Hershey, PA.

Reid, Tori. 2016. Enable Android's Secret Right-to-Left Layout If You're Left Handed. *Lifehacker*. ed., Melissa Kirsch, Accessed December 13, 2016. http://lifehacker.com/enable-androids-secret-right-to-left-layout-if-youre-le-1676267178, Gizmodo Media, New York.

Section508. 2016. Technology Accessibility Playbook | Section508.gov. Accessed December 13, 2016. https://www.section508.gov/content/technology-accessibility-playbook.

Silfverberg, Miika, I. Scott MacKenzie, and Panu Korhonen. 2000. Predicting Text Entry Speed on Mobile Phones. In Proceedings of the SIGCHI Conference on Human Factors in Computing Systems—CHI '00. doi:10.1145/332040.332044.

Synchrony Financial. 2016. MySynchrony Consumer Financing | Synchrony Bank. Accessed December 15, 2016. https://www.mysynchrony.com/mysyf/home.html?

Twitter. 2016. Sign up. Accessed December 20, 2016. https://twitter.com/signup?lang=en.

U.S. Web Design Standards. 2016. U.S. Web Design Standards Documentation | UI Components. 2016. Accessed December 13, 2016. https://standards.usa.gov/.

W3C. 2016. Understanding Success Criterion 1.4.3 | Understanding WCAG 2.0. Accessed December 10, 2016. https://www.w3.org/TR/UNDERSTANDING-WCAG20/visual-audio-contrast-contrast.html.

Ziggo. 2016. Account Aanmaken | Mijn Ziggo | Ziggo. Accessed December 20, 2016. https://www.ziggo.nl/mijn/registreren/stap1/.

12

Error Prevention and Security

Web Browsers
Customizing: Control of Security Settings
References

The set of protocols and guidelines for error prevention and security varies with the type of software and system development underneath the interface. This chapter mentions a few examples of software system structure for web and mobile applications. Designers should know where the certifications and security icons are located so that they can design a more realistic interface for user testing. These details are usually implemented and revised by a cyber-security team, which provides expert knowledge about any security threats. Cybersecurity is usually an ongoing process, with the team regularly checking on online accounts such as email, active secure sites, or apps where the content is being exchanged constantly. Designers must design interfaces that give their users a sense of security.

Web Browsers

Security Icon

The URL or information bar always has a lock icon, usually green (Figure 12.1), showing the security of the present web page. When the user enters a dangerous zone, the lock will turn red as a warning. Usually, "green" pages are protected by Secure Sockets Layer (SSL)/Transport Layer Security (TLS) or another protocol of similar

Figure 12.1

Google Docs, an online application that allows users to edit and save content securely. The user senses security from the green lock icon in the browser bar.

value; the example in Figure 12.1 is using HTTPS, or HyperText Transfer Protocol over SSL, which encrypts the content so it cannot be read by anyone other than the user (Instant SSL, 2016). Make sure that the web pages are protected by security protocols, especially for online accounts handling monetary transactions or any type of delicate and private information, such as an email account. Show this type of visual security indication to make the user feel safe interacting with the page.

Undo

When the user deletes a message or any other data, the interface should provide an option to undo that action. For example, Outlook Mail (Figure 12.2), which is part of hotmail.com, has a very helpful Undo button to go one step backwards.

Another great technique is to place the undo option in a pop-up window, as seen in Figure 12.3.

Figure 12.2

Undo option on the right side of the main menu of Outlook Mail. (Courtesy of Outlook.com—Microsoft Free Personal Email, 2016, https://outlook.live.com/owa/.)

Figure 12.3

In a mobile application, a pop-up window might be more convenient because of screen-size limitations. (Courtesy of Apple Inc., Cupertino, CA, USA, 2016, https://developer.apple.com/ios/human-interface-guidelines/interaction/undo-and-redo/.)

12. Error Prevention and Security

Misspellings

When searching or typing, a tool often helps us with spelling. In Figure 12.4, Google Search has corrected the spelling and is giving us a link to search for the originally typed word. This saves us time if we truly made a mistake. Possible words are suggested automatically as we type (Figure 12.5).

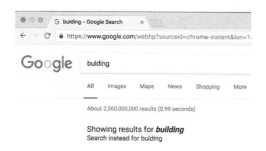

Figure 12.4

Google search results with auto-corrected spelling. (Courtesy of Google, Mountain View, CA, USA, 2016, http://www.google.com/logos/doodles/2016/winter-solstice-2016-northern-hemisphere-4788310770712576-hp2x.gif.)

Figure 12.5

Google search tool with auto-filling option. (Courtesy of Google, Mountain View, CA, USA, 2016, http://www.google.com/logos/doodles/2016/winter-solstice-2016-northern-hemisphere-4788310770712576-hp2x.gif.)

Autosave

Automatic file saving—or *autosave*—can be a lifesaver in any application, especially in emergencies, when the software crashes suddenly without the user clicking Save (Figure 12.6). Autosave is extremely necessary for any interface, where the user is constantly changing, updating, or revising files. Users do not have time to keep saving files every 5 minutes.

Captcha

Captcha (Figure 12.7), a free project launched in 2000 by Lui von Ahn, Manuel Blum, Nicholas Hopper, and John Langford of Carnegie Mellon University,

Figure 12.6

"All changes saved in Drive" and "Saving..." are indications of autosaving in Google Docs. (Courtesy of Google, 2016, http://www.google.com.)

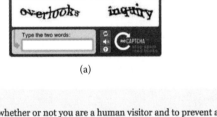

(a)

CAPTCHA

This question is for testing whether or not you are a human visitor and to prevent automated spam submissions.

Math question *

10 + 4 =

Solve this simple math problem and enter the result. E.g. for 1+3, enter 4.

(b)

Figure 12.7

Captcha examples with both (a) words and (b) numbers. (Courtesy of uxpa, 2016, https://uxpa.org/membership/global-sustaining-member.)

stands for "completely automated public Turing test to tell computers and humans apart." Possible to implement on any website, visit http://www.captcha. net for more information. Captcha recognizes whether the agent accessing information is a robot or a human, which can protect against a wide range of scams or spam in website registrations or online evaluations.

404 Pages

Error 404 pages, which are shown when a user-requested page cannot be found, should appear as visually friendly as possible. Users will otherwise automatically close the browser window because they perceive that the website lacks security and reliability. If instead the web page provides a friendly and accessibly designed 404 page, as in the example in Figure 12.8, it makes the user feel safe and provides links to elsewhere on the website, such as Home, About, Contact, or Search.

Figure 12.8

404 page example. (Courtesy of Behance, 2016, https://www.behance.net/gallery/10120897/Pigeon.)

Error Windows

Windows that appear to let the user know that something has gone wrong should convey friendliness, not terror. Work on the copywriting inside error windows until they encourage the user and do not make the user feel uncomfortable or unsafe (Figure 12.9).

Figure 12.9

CreateTextFile Error! (Courtesy of Silent Runners, 2016, http://www.silentrunners.org/faq.html.)

Password Errors

When users create accounts or change passwords, many mistakes and a lot of frustration can be resolved through a careful process from design to testing, including copywriting the interface content (Figure 12.10).

Figure 12.10

Logging into hotmail.com, with the error resulting from typing more characters than needed in the password field. (Courtesy of The Windows Club, 2015, http://www.thewindowsclub.com/maximum-length-of-password-windows-10.)

Security Branding

The branding of security should be consistent and not compete with the main branding and identity of the interface (Figure 12.11) but should be a smaller part of the entire interface. Though small, it is an extremely important part of the interface because it makes users feel secure enough to risk their personal information. Certified icons and other visual elements can emphasize secure content and security tools, varying from interface to interface. Some interfaces might need just a login page, while others, such as an Apple iPad, may need a more complex level of security settings.

Unprotected app

Protected app

Protected app with custom icon

Figure 12.11

Security branding in an app icon. (Courtesy of Metzger, S., 2016, Security Branding Your App Drives Recognition and Trust, https://www.bluecedar.com/blog/securitybranding-your-app-drives-recognition-and-trust.)

Custom Designs

Interfaces will less easily become scammed if the design is custom and includes a custom typeface, identity, layout, and visual certifications that reinforce security.

Typefaces

For large-budget projects, investing in a custom typeface is very beneficial. A typeface solely used by a company will automatically confer a higher level of recognition and trust from the user's point of view.

12. Error Prevention and Security

Icons

Security symbols in an interface, from logos to menu icons, should be consistent in terms of weight and location. Users rely on security symbols such as lock icons or a certified logo, so these reinforce the reliability of the interface. In addition, color and visual design consistency are extremely important (Figure 12.12).

Figure 12.12

Security icon set. (Courtesy of Noun Project, 2016, https://thenounproject.com.)

Pop-Ups

Pop-ups can become very annoying. If something randomly appears in front of a user's eyes while they are reading, this type of interaction can be surprising enough and users can be afraid enough that they will exit the interface completely. After all, pop-ups could represent a virus or someone trying to retrieve your information.

Blinking

Anything blinking on an interface will make users feel less secure about the interface, because many scam websites have images or text blinking trying to gain attention.

Opening an Interstitial Display before Application

When an application opens, it can be necessary to show some type of graphical information about copyright and other information that restates the trustworthiness of the application (Figure 12.13).

Figure 12.13

Photoshop application opening, before entering the interface. (Courtesy of Adobe Photoshop, 2016, http://www.adobe.com/products/photoshop.html.)

Closing Pop-Up Windows

When users finish with an application, website, or other software, show that they are done completely. Especially after asking a user to fill out a form, make sure the interface has a closing statement and a reassuring button that makes the user aware that they are exiting the program correctly and safely. Include statements such as "you have exited the program; log in here again" or "your purchase has been submitted, thank you and you can close the window now" or a reassuring statement, such as "are you sure you want to close?"

Glitches

Errors can and should be prevented during interface testing. Data breaches or interface errors caught too late can cost millions to repair all losses.

According to a global data breach study done by IBM and the Ponemon Institute in June 2016, 383 companies in 12 countries suffered data breaches, each of which costs around $4 million. This represents a cost increase of 29% since 2013. Each stolen record costs around $158. Making mistakes by not providing the right interface security can cost millions. This responsibility belongs not only to visual design but also to the development process and final testing. These data highlight the importance of testing and visual interface security literacy so that users may be made aware of whether or not they are in a safe zone.

Customizing: Control of Security Settings

Some interfaces provide an entire section to control security settings, including Wi-Fi security, backup, locking, and other tools, depending on user requirements. The example in Figure 12.14 provides various options very clearly, with consistent branding and iconography throughout.

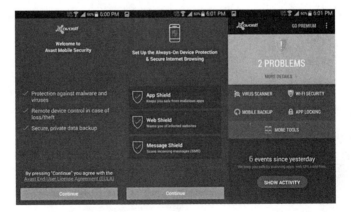

Figure 12.14

Avast antivirus interface for Android smartphones. (Courtesy of Technology Bites, 2015, http://www.teknobites.com/best-free-android-antivirus-to-secure-your-android-smartphone/.)

References

Apple Inc. 2016. Undo and Redo—Interaction—iOS Human Interface Guidelines. Accessed April 21, 2017. https://developer.apple.com/ios/human-interface-guidelines/interaction/undo-and-redo/.

Behance. 2016. Accessed April 21, 2017. https://www.behance.net/gallery/10120897/Pigeon.

Google. 2016. Accessed April 21, 2017. http://www.google.com/logos/doodles/2016/winter-solstice-2016-northern-hemisphere-4788310770712576-hp2x.gif.

Instant SSL. 2016. HTTP to HTTPS | What Is a HTTPS Certificate. Accessed April 21, 2017. https://www.instantssl.com/ssl-certificate-products/https.html.

Metzger, Sharon. 2016. Security Branding Your App Drives Recognition and Trust. Accessed April 21, 2017. https://www.bluecedar.com/blog/security-branding-your-app-drives-recognition-and-trust.

Noun Project. 2016. *Noun Project.* Accessed April 21, 2017. https://thenounproject.com.

Outlook.com—Microsoft Free Personal Email. 2016. Accessed April 21, 2017. https://outlook.live.com/owa/.

Silent Runners. 2016. FAQ Accessed April 21, 2017. http://www.silentrunners.org/faq.html.

Technology Bites. 2015. Best Free Android Antivirus to Secure Your Android Smartphone. 2015. Accessed April 21, 2017. http://www.teknobites.com/best-free-android-antivirus-to-secure-your-android-smartphone/.

uxpa. 2016. Choose Your Membership Level | User Experience Professionals Association. Accessed April 21, 2017. https://uxpa.org/membership/global-sustaining-member.

The Windows Club. 2015. AnandK@TWC. What Is the Maximum Length of Password in Windows 10? Accessed April 21, 2017. http://www.thewindowsclub.com/maximum-length-of-password-windows-10.

13

Usability, Testing, and Acceptance

This chapter introduces usability, testing, and acceptance. For further, more detailed reading, explore the list of recommended books in the Appendix.

This chapter will cover the three important stages of defining a successful prototype: (1) usability, which moves to (2) user testing the design, the results of which lead to (3) the final acceptance of the user.

Usability

According to the international standard ISO 9241-210, design concepts, even at early stages, should be evaluated for refinement in more depth and detail to fulfill user needs better.

Use the method of task modeling and simulations to understand what people want. Learn how to design for your users by learning their behavior and needs from the beginning of the project. Using task-modeling methods, we give direct tasks to the user, understanding from their responses to the interface whether it is effective and easy for them to comply with the requested tasks. Simulations, also known as *prototypes*, are essential in the process, from paper prototyping to digitally developed simulations, as we have discussed.

Affordances, Signifiers, and Instructional Manuals

Affordances

Psychologist James J. Gibson created this term to describe the relationship between an object and a person, or even between animals and their surroundings. Affordances can be directly applied to visual experiences in two-, three-, and four-dimensional worlds. For example, 2-year-olds cannot afford to use a desktop computer, but they can afford to use a smartphone because of its size, given apps suiting their age. Study a person's affordances with the following questions: How? What? Why? (Figures 13.1 and 13.2).

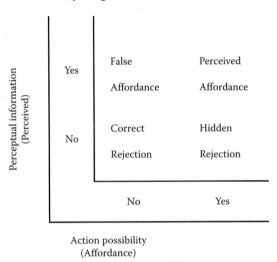

Figure 13.1

Diagram showing false and perceived affordances, including correct and hidden rejections. (Courtesy of Interaction Design Foundation, 2016, https://www.interaction-design.org/index.php/literature/book/the-encyclo pedia-of-human-computer-interaction-2nd-ed/affordances.)

Types of Affordances

1. *Explicit affordance*: If a button gives written affordance, it is very clear, such as "submit button" or "next" (Figure 13.3).
2. *Pattern affordance*: Pattern affordance is necessary throughout any type of interface, keeping the UI organized and allowing easy navigation and recognition. Examples include the hamburger menu, the interface's color branding, and logos (Figure 13.4).
3. *Hidden affordance*: Users are very used to hidden affordances that appear when they click a drop-down menu or a slide gallery (Figure 13.5). This affordance helps designers create containers of larger content that still reveal the content to the user in an orderly manner.

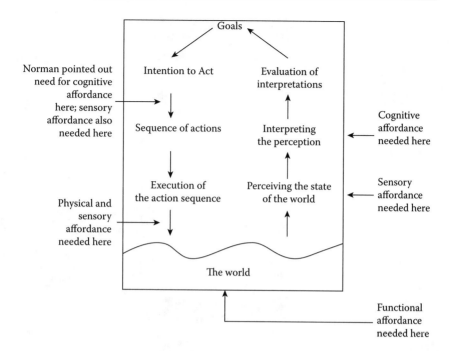

Figure 13.2

Norman's stages-of-action model. (Courtesy of Hartson, R., *Behav. Inform. Tech.*, 22, 315–338, 2003.)

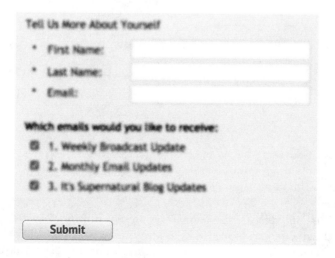

Figure 13.3

Online submission form. (Courtesy of Roth, S., 2016, Thank You!—Sid Roth—It's Supernatural, *Sid Roth—It's Supernatural*, http://sidroth.org/quick-registration-thank-you/.)

Figure 13.4

Hamburger menu on Amazon Android app. (Courtesy of Thompson, R., et al., 2016, *Amazon Shopping—Android Apps on Google Play*, https://play.google.com/store/apps/details?id=com.amazon.mShop.android.shopping&hl=en.)

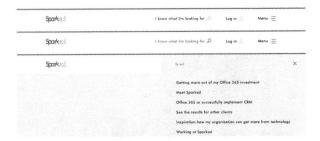

Figure 13.5

Search tool hides the typing tool for search. (Courtesy of Sparked, 2016, http://www.sparked.nl/.)

1. *False affordance*: False affordances are not usually created on purpose. Usually, they are broken links or advertisements that say "click here," or, as in Figure 13.6, have an icon representing closing that does not do anything.
2. *Metaphorical affordance*: Metaphors are very helpful affordances, with icons guiding us directly to the functionality (Figure 13.7). Examples include a shopping cart, a pen, a printer icon, a trash can, or even a heart.

Figure 13.6

The Close button looks like an affordance, but it is only a sample version of the button. (Courtesy of Twardowski, O., *"Flavour Extended" by Oliver Twardowski*, Iconfinder, 2016, https://www.iconfinder.com/icons/14753/button_delete_red_icon.)

Figure 13.7

Trash icon. (From TutsPlus.com, 2016a, https://cdn.tutsplus.com/mac/authors/jacob-penderworth/Trash-icon-retina.png.)

Figure 13.8

Interface showing a list of broken links. (Courtesy of wpmudev, 2016b, https://premium.wpmudev.org/blog/wp-content/uploads/2011/12/broken-links2.jpg.)

3. *Negative affordance*: This affordance alerts you when something is inactive. It could be an icon, content, broken link, or even sections with which you are not supposed to interact because they are presently inactive (Figure 13.8). In addition, if logging into an account, without your password it will not allow access.

Conceptual Models

Signifiers are communication devices. The term *signifiers* contains the word *sign*, indicating visual symbolism.

Don Norman encourages designers to use the term *signifiers* instead of *affordances* for visual cues in interfaces (Norman 2013). Signifiers are everywhere in interfaces, as the word itself stands for *sign*, meaning an action that conveys culturally specific information. The linguist Ferdinand de Saussure distinguished two components: the signifier (sound–image) and the signified (concept). From this basis, visual experiences have now evolved to more complex systems due to culture and visual communication through interfaces.

The basic concept starts as follows.

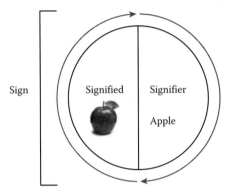

Figure 13.9

Diagram representing *sign, signified,* and *signifier.*

According to Saussure, all signs must have a signified and a signifier. It is important to understand this concept because interfaces—indeed, any 100% visual communication—must have the complete form. The signifier must be something visual that is extremely recognizable by the user. Meanwhile, the signified part is the concept that is represented, which could be contextual (Figure 13.9).

Examples of combined signifiers and affordances in interfaces follow (Figure 13.10).

Visible versus Invisible

A signifier with a missing affordance is shown in Figure 13.11. The search icon is visible, but the bar to type in the words is hidden. The user will automatically click the search icon (a signifier), and the search box will appear right after (a hidden affordance).

Signifiers Are Critical for UI Systems

Signifiers are the essence of interfaces, without which we cannot communicate visually at all. Only through signifiers can we create successful visual experiences.

13. Usability, Testing, and Acceptance

Figure 13.10

Diagram showing parts of the Twitter interface. There are various signs, such as the Twitter logo and the Like and Reply icons at the bottom.

Figure 13.11

Search bar with hidden affordance. (Courtesy of Codrops, 2016, http://tympanus.net/Tutorials/ExpandingSearchBar/.)

Signifiers are everywhere, with examples including icons, glyphs, color, images, and structure.

Controls

Instructional Manuals

Instructional manuals are needed for visual experiences in a larger system containing several affordances and hidden signifiers that are revealed through multiple steps to execute tasks and functions (Figure 13.12). A manual is especially needed if the interface requires some settings and programming, such as a house app control or a car interface (Figure 13.13).

Be aware of the positive impact of giving an instructional manual to the user. The manual will provide the user a sense of safety and security when using the interface, as the user will be guided by clear, direct, and straight-to-the-point steps. Manuals may be video, audio, or print.

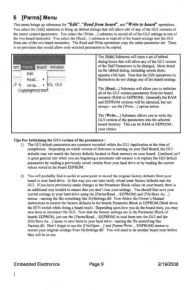

Figure 13.12

Manual for managing an interface step by step.

Figure 13.13

Coleman, Screen shot of a Manual showing how complex can be a manual because of the layers that a Graphical User Interface can have.

13. Usability, Testing, and Acceptance

Testing

Testing is incredibly important when making revisions and edits to interfaces. For more information on usability testing, see Chapter 3, which explains in detail various types of user evaluations. In addition, I provide a list of books in the Appendix that solely concentrate on testing, explaining usability testing in much further detail. Another very helpful source is ISO 29119, which provides a series of techniques for testing.

There are usually several testing instances from the creation of an interface to the end. According to Don Norman, each test execution comprises seven stages:

1. What do I want to accomplish?
2. What are my alternatives?
3. What can I do now?
4. How do I do it?
5. What happened?
6. What does it mean?
7. Is it OK? Have I accomplished my goal?

Every time we execute a test, we should follow all seven steps above in an orderly manner to structure that test.

Norman's Gulf of Execution and Evaluation

Norman's gulf of execution and evaluation resolve and shorten the time required for testing, facilitating the process of execution and evaluation (Figures 13.14 and 13.15). Seven stages of action are as follows:

1. Forming the goal
2. Forming the intention
3. Specifying an action sequence
4. Executing an action
5. Perceiving the state of the world
6. Interpreting the state of the world
7. Evaluating the outcome

The Gulf of Execution

Execution > Goal > Evaluation

Figure 13.14

System flow of execution, goal, and evaluation.

Goals

Evaluation of
interpretations

Intention to act

Evaluation · Interpreting the perception · Sequence of actions · Execution

Perceiving the state of the world

Execution of the action sequence

World

Figure 13.15

Norman's gulf of execution and evaluation. This approach is a very simple idea for how to approach testing or analysis. First, you set goals, and then you jump into the world, acting and executing the tasks and then evaluating, perceiving, and evaluating the results.

Assessing the State of the Gulf and whether It Matches the Goal

Ten rules for good design according to Dieter Rams are as follows:

1. Good design is innovative.
2. Good design makes a product useful.
3. Good design is aesthetic.
4. Good design makes a product understandable.
5. Good design is unobtrusive.
6. Good design is honest.
7. Good design is long-lasting.
8. Good design is thorough down to the last detail.
9. Good design is environmentally friendly.
10. Good design involves as little design as possible.

When testing prototypes, as mentioned earlier, constantly identify any questions that come up and resolve any problems. Moving to the final development process does not mean testing is done. Actually, to have a final, successful interface, more testing is very much needed to refine the developed version further before sending it out to the market.

Quick reminder of the stages of prototyping are as follows:

1. Sketches
2. Paper

3. Digital (using a basic prototyping tool)
4. Medium fidelity (quick prototyping tool with more interactive options)
5. High level (an early developed version)
6. Video (showing a step-by-step prototype, including user documentation, which could be very helpful for investors, users, etc.)
7. Coding a prototype (final developed version, 2–6 days or more, depending on complexity)

Acceptance

The Difference between User Acceptance Testing and User Testing

User testing is a very important process of testing interfaces right before their release by the designer.

UAT, or *user acceptance testing*, is usually the last phase of testing, done by the client. Only external users and the client interact with the fully developed interface at this point. This rigorous process specifically tests whether the interface contradicts any of the rules and requirements it provides the user. During UAT, only graphical interface mistakes may be found, not code glitches or software development failures.

For example, what happens if a user puts the wrong information into a form or submits it incorrectly? UAT looks at any type of error a user might make. In summary, UAT looks to see whether the interface is bulletproof against user mistakes. After UAT, the interface is ready to go to the market.

Overall, during UAT, the interface design team must be alert and ready to make any last-minute changes before the interface is ready for public availability.

Watch Out for the Bugs!

Due to the lack of consistent user acceptance testing, many software programs have had to deal with bugs. In 2002, a study commissioned by the National Institute of Standards and Technology found that software bugs cost the US economy alone $59.5 billion every year. The study showed that proper testing could eliminate $22.2 billion of this loss.

One of the biggest bugs cost Knight's $44 million in 30 minutes (Raygun 2014). The shares lost 75% two days after the software went onto the market with the bug. An algorithmic problem sent 150 different stocks into spasms, a problem that could have been resolved before release with rigorous testing.

Thus, every step in the process when creating interfaces, software, and applications is essential. Constant revisions, check-ups, and testing will help ensure success and reliability. As we live in an online world with all our information out there, it is extremely important to keep the functionality of an interface up to date, including keeping the security features always visible in the interface.

Some interfaces can be for extremely serious applications, such as medical equipment. In cases where lives are at stake, it is very important to have no bugs at the end of testing.

References

Codrops. 2016. Expanding Search Bar Deconstructed. Accessed December 16. http://tympanus.net/Tutorials/ExpandingSearchBar/.

Hartson, Rex. 2003. Cognitive, Physical, Sensory, and Functional Affordances in Interaction Design. *Behaviour & Information Technology* 22(5): 315–338.

Interaction Design Foundation. 2016. *Affordances: The Encyclopedia of Human-Computer Interaction*, 2nd Edition. Accessed December 16. https://www.interaction-design.org/index.php/literature/book/the-encyclopedia-of-human-computer-interaction-2nd-ed/affordances.

ISO. 2013. ISO/IEC/IEEE 29119-1:2013—Software and Systems Engineering—Software Testing—Part 1: Concepts and Definitions. Accessed April 21, 2017. http://www.iso.org/iso/home/store/catalogue_tc/catalogue_detail.htm?csnumber=45142.

ISO. 2015. ISO/IEC/IEEE 29119-4:2015—Software and Systems Engineering—Software Testing—Part 4: Test Techniques. Accessed April 21, 2017. http://www.iso.org/iso/home/store/catalogue_tc/catalogue_detail.htm?csnumber=60245.

Norman, Donald A. 2013. *The Design of Everyday Things: Revised and Expanded Edition*. Basic Books, New York.

Raygun. 2014. 10 of the Most Costly Software Errors in History. Accessed May 29. https://raygun.com/blog/2014/05/10-costly-software-errors-history/.

Roth, Sid. 2016. Thank You!—Sid Roth—It's Supernatural. *Sid Roth—It's Supernatural*. Accessed December 19. http://sidroth.org/quick-registration-thank-you/.

Sparked. 2016. Accessed December 19. http://www.sparked.nl/.

Thompson, Rayna, Sharon Wade, N. Bilal, Kindel Culver, Dolourous Haze, C. Tony, Shaterica Vaughn, et al. 2016. *Amazon Shopping—Android Apps on Google Play*. Accessed December 19. https://play.google.com/store/apps/details?id=com.amazon.mShop.android.shopping&hl=en.

TutsPlus.com. 2016a. Accessed December 19. https://cdn.tutsplus.com/mac/authors/jacob-penderworth/Trash-icon-retina.png.

Twardowski, Oliver. 2016. "Flavour Extended" by Oliver Twardowski. *Iconfinder*. Accessed December 19. https://www.iconfinder.com/icons/14753/button_delete_red_icon.

Webdesigner Depot. 2015. 6 Types of Digital Affordance That Impact Your UX | Webdesigner Depot. Accessed April 7. http://www.webdesignerdepot.com/2015/04/6-types-of-digital-affordance-that-impact-your-ux/.

wpmudev. 2016b. Accessed December 19. https://premium.wpmudev.org/blog/wp-content/uploads/2011/12/broken-links2.jpg.

14

Designing for Large Interfaces

Larger devices do not have an interface standard. Instead, this medium is flexible; consider the client's budget and goal and proceed from there to the limitations and possibilities.

Large interfaces can be designed at three different levels: personal, participatory, and environmental. A personal-level interface could be the size of a tablet, desktop (Figure 14.1), or anything else that interacts one on one with users. Participatory interfaces are geared toward users who are sharing and interacting with each other on a large screen, usually placed on a wall or table (Figure 14.2). In addition, large interfaces may have two purposes: sharing information to educate and a playful interface to entertain.

Narrowing down unlimited possibilities may require adding an engineer, industrial designer, or even an interior designer to the project. If the interface is outside, in a public space, the project may need an environmental designer or architect. When on a larger scale, these projects require extra professional help because not only the interface but also a physical product is being designed to interact with user(s) and the environment.

Figure 14.1

Poverty Tracker | Robin Hood, a project of the Columbia Population Research Center. (Courtesy of Poverty Tracker, http://povertytracker.robinhood.org/.)

Human Factors and Ergonomics

Human factors are essential to guide and set parameters in height, width, distance, and depth between the interface and the user.

Important questions to ask to provide some context for human factors include the following:

- What is the purpose of the interaction?
- Will only one user interact or a group?

Figure 14.2

Pentagram, Interactive installation at the SCAD Museum of Art. (Courtesy of Pentagram, 2016, http://www.pentagram.com /#/blog/37686?our_works=1541,all,rel.)

- Is this purely entertainment or is it educational?
- How much space do we need?
- How is the user positioned during interaction: sitting, dancing, standing, something else?

Ergonomics and Limitations

Figure 14.3 represents human visual physiology.

The physiology of the eye allows binocular vision of 62 degrees turning to the left and the right, but symbols can be recognized only from 5 to 30 degrees. These measurements are aligned to the viewer's line of sight. The physiology

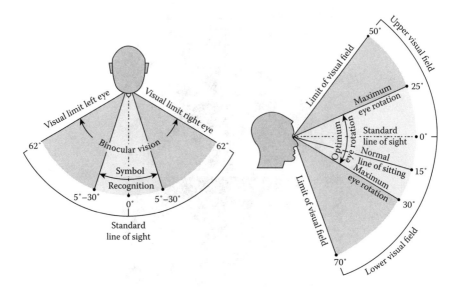

Figure 14.3

Visual angle limitations. (Courtesy of Extron Electronics, CA, USA, 2016a, http://www. extron.com/company/article.aspx?id=environconhumanfact&tab=technology.)

of the eye has also limitations looking up and down. The upper visual field reaches up to 50 degrees, while the lower field reaches to 70 degrees. Concerning eye rotation, the normal line of sight when sitting is between 0 and 15 degrees, with maximum eye rotation of 30 degrees. In design, these guidelines provide restrictions and limitations on legibility. An interface that follows them will be more effective than one that does not.

Distance

Before deciding on type size and image layout, the designer must know who will be reading and interacting with the interface: a child, a digital-native adult, an elderly person? The type of user will help to narrow down possibilities and options in colors, type size, and branding (Figure 14.4).

Ambience

The conditions of lighting (Figure 14.5) are also important and vary with the size of the interface and nature of users' interaction with it. Appropriate lighting conditions are different for screens compared with a projection. An engineer and an A/V designer should help make final decisions so the interface can be viewed effectively.

Brightness and contrast (Figure 14.6) must be well balanced in the space, which will vary depending on the interface's physical placement. Is it on a wall,

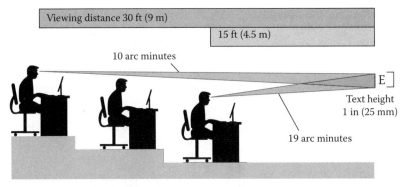

Font size is acceptable for nearest viewer, but too small for extended viewing by furthest viewer

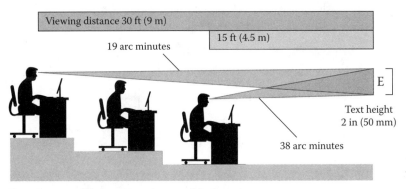

Font size acceptable for nearest viewer and furthest viewer

Figure 14.4

Visual legibility limitations. (Courtesy of Extron Electronics, CA, USA, 2016b, http://www.extron.com/company/article.aspx?id=videowallfontsize.)

in a table, or something else? For example (Figure 14.7), Second Story created an exhibit for the Coca-Cola Company based on a late-nineteenth-century appearance of vintage objects kept in shelves and drawers. In the context of the exhibit, this design idea reinforced the main idea of the exhibit, that the recipe of Coca-Cola is a well-kept secret. The user interacts with the drawers, but to the surprise of visitors who open this drawer, however, they find a screen on another security monitor. They see themselves from an unusual angle, directly overhead. Their image is scanned, and then amazingly they are transformed into 3D computer data. Suddenly, a mysterious character who keeps cropping up in the exhibit media, the man in the hat, walks through the scene. When visitors look around, he's not really there! (Second Story 2016b)

Some stationary and environmental interfaces are replacing analog types of machines. For example, the LinkNYC project has replaced phone booths

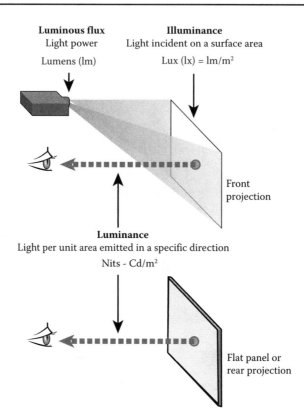

Figure 14.5

Visual illuminance limitations.

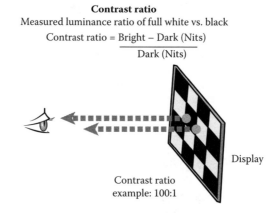

Figure 14.6

Visual contrast limitations.

14. Designing for Large Interfaces

Figure 14.7

Security drawer system designed by Second Story. (Courtesy of Second Story, 2016b, http://secondstory.com/project/search/secret-formula-security-system-drawer?q=The%20Coca-Cola%20Company.)

Figure 14.8

Goodbye phone booths, LinkNYC. (Courtesy of Intersection, 2016, http://citybridge.com.)

Figure 14.9

Human interaction with the interface, LinkNYC. (Courtesy of Intersection, 2016, http://citybridge.com.)

(Figure 14.8) with stations (Figure 14.9) that provide Internet, Wi-Fi, a USB charger, and access to a phone to call anyone in the United States. All these services and much more are provided for free at about 10,000 stations placed throughout the New York City (Figure 14.10). Ads displayed on the large screen on the side of the booth are paying for this service, which is expected to generate revenue of $500 million in the first 12 years (NYC 2016).

Figure 14.10

Silicon NYC, Nightlife with LinkNYC in New York City. (Courtesy of Intersection, 2016, http://silicon.nyc/local-business-advertising-linknyc-wifi/.)

Figure 14.11

Hermes Miami. (Courtesy of Second Story, 2016a, http://secondstory.com/project/browse/featured-work/hermes-miami.)

Interfaces as Entertainment

Hermes Miami explores the interaction of the physical body with the interface. Figure 14.11 shows how users make gestures, with the result of the interaction recorded in one digital collage that you can receive as a memory of the event.

Information Design in Large Interfaces

The Poverty Tracker (Figure 14.12) was designed for the large-screen web. When a user accesses it on a small screen, the interface informs the user that the experience would be better on a larger screen.

Figure 14.12

Poverty Tracker | Robin Hood, a project of the Columbia Population Research Center, designed by Fathom.

The Poverty Tracker website has a gridded layout with information that could be extremely difficult to understand from raw data alone. It shows percentages of overall poverty in New York City by household type, education, age, gender, and race in comparison to the percentage suffering from chronic health problems like asthma, diabetes, and hypertension. The data may be clearly distinguished thanks to the visual design.

Participatory Interface Design

The table installation in Figure 14.12 allows more than 20 people to interact with the interface at once. The table provides on-screen playing cards that allow users to interact with information about the museum and events, along with showcasing the museum's collections.

References

Extron Electronics. 2016a. Environmental Considerations and Human Factors for Videowall Design | Extron. Accessed December 23, 2016. http://www.extron.com/company/article.aspx?id=environconhumanfact&tab=technology.

Extron Electronics. 2016b. Font Size and Legibility for Videowall Content | Extron. Accessed December 23, 2016. http://www.extron.com/company/article.aspx?id=videowallfontsize.

Intersection. 2016. CityBridge | LinkNYC. *CityBridge | LinkNYC*. Accessed December 22, 2016. http://citybridge.com.

NYC. 2016. DoITT—LinkNYC. 2016. Accessed December 22, 2016. https://www1.nyc.gov/site/doitt/initiatives/linknyc.page.

Pentagram. 2016. Accessed December 22, 2016. http://www.pentagram.com/#/
blog/37686?our_works=1541,all,rel.

Second Story. 2016a A Man's World, Miami | Featured Work | Second Story.
Accessed December 22, 2016. http://secondstory.com/project/browse/
featured-work/hermes-miami.

Second Story. 2016b. Security System Drawer | Search | Second Story. Accessed
December 23, 2016. http://secondstory.com/project/search/secret-formula-
security-system-drawer?q=The%20Coca-Cola%20Company.

15

Designing for Small Devices

Interfaces for small devices, such as smartphones, tablets, and watches, require a more personal connection between the interface and the user. There are millions of such apps, with more every day because of user demand. Apps are children's e-books, social media, tools, games, and more. The world today is saturated with apps.

Several platforms allow building apps, each of which has guidelines that interface designers and developers must analyze very carefully. Every platform is a whole new challenge, with limitations and standards to understand. For example, some platforms do not permit hamburger menus, requiring navigation to stay at the bottom of the screen. All of these restrictions need to be learned and researched before designing an interface.

The best angle of viewing rotation is 15–30 degrees, beyond which it becomes harder to read (Figure 15.1). With more rotation, the interface content is placed in horizontal perspective.

Mobile phones and tablets have a hierarchical order on the screen (Figure 15.2). It is harder for users to interact with the sections of the screen in yellow on the figure because these sections require both hands to interact with a handheld device. The most accessible region is toward the bottom of the device.

The children's game Yibu (Figures 15.3 through 15.6) involves five crafted wooden toys containing sensors, each of which interacts with the game.

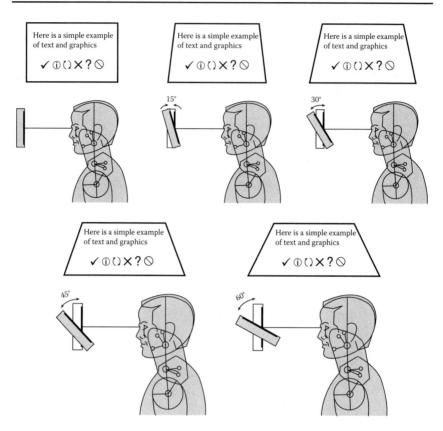

Figure 15.1

Various angles at which a small screen is accessed. (Courtesy of Bridge Design Inc., San Francisco, CA, USA, 2015, http://bridgedesign.com/touch-screen-ergonomics/.)

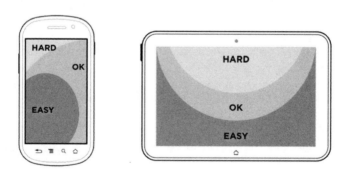

Figure 15.2

Interaction regions of users on mobile devices, from hard to easy. (Courtesy of UCOP, Oakland, CA, USA, 2016, http://www.ucop.edu/risk-services/loss-prevention-control/ergonomics/ergo-mobile.html.)

Figure 15.3

Physical objects that interact with the Yibu app.

Figure 15.4

Yibu game with physical objects.

Figure 15.5

Child interacting with the physical toy.

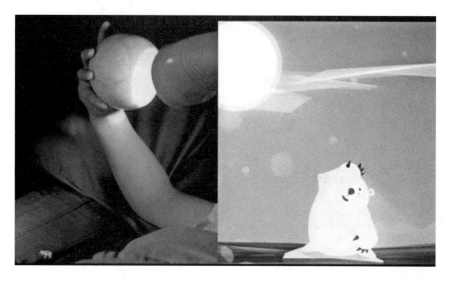

Figure 15.6

Yibu game app designed by Frog Design. Child interacting with the physical toy and the view (on the left) and the outcome visually in the app (on the right). (Courtesy of Frog, 2016, http://www.frogdesign.com/work/yibu.html.)

Every time the toy is placed in the sun or the cold, the character in the interface also changes environment. The interface uses bright colors for its illustrations, which enriches children's visual experience of the app.

Part of the Reach Higher initiative was to guide students to take better advantage of federal support to go to secondary school. The Up Next app (Figure 15.7) gives young students step-by-step information on filling out forms such as the Free Application for Federal Student Aid (FAFSA), with deadlines and much more. The app interacts with the user's text messaging to create a FAFSA ID, and the interface is user-friendly, with a design strategy focused on high-school students. According to a study by Huge, 88% of teenagers have smartphones, 90% exchange texts, 92% go online daily, and teenagers typically receive 30 text messages daily. These data suggested to Huge that they could reach a huge number of teenagers across the United States through this app.

Streaks (Figures 15.8 through 15.13) is an iPhone and Apple Watch app. It provides many setting choices for color palette. The app helps its users create consistency in their daily routine, from setting a schedule for eating meals to walking the dog or brushing their teeth. With very simple functionalities, the app can make our daily lives much more productive and consistent.

Figure 15.7

Up Next app designed and developed by Huge Inc. (Courtesy of Huge, Brooklyn, NY, USA, 2016, http://www.hugeinc.com/case-study/up-next.)

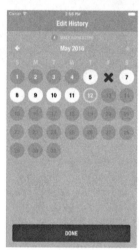

Figure 15.8

Streaks, designed by Zervaas Enterprises. (Courtesy of STREAKS, 2016a, https://streaksapp.com/.)

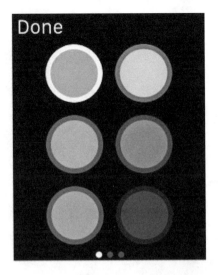
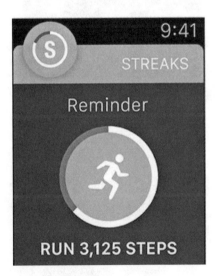

Figure 15.9

Streaks, designed by Zervaas Enterprises. Apple Watch app shown here. The app can give you reminders and help you keep up with your daily routines and activities. (Courtesy of STREAKS, 2016b, https://streaksapp.com/.)

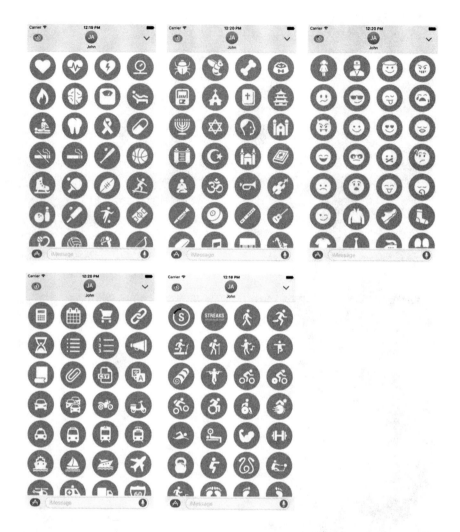

Figure 15.10

Streaks provides its own custom message icons for Apple iMessage. (Courtesy of STREAKS, 2016c, https://streaksapp.com/.)

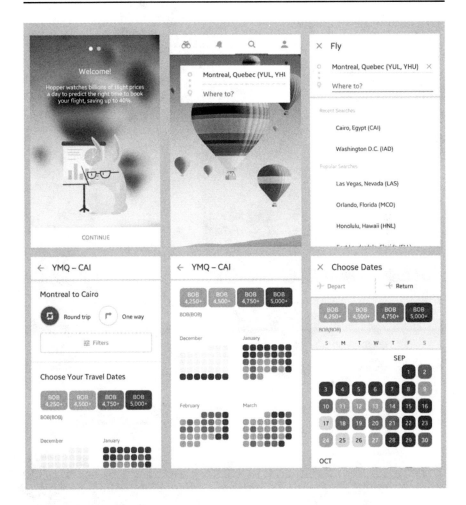

Figure 15.11

Hopper is a mobile app that sends users alerts when airplane tickets go up or down in price and predicts the best time to buy a ticket for a certain flight. Using a set of four colors, green, yellow, orange, and red, the app uses green as the cheapest price and red as the highest. The screenshot shows color-coded dates with less or more expensive tickets. This app gathers constantly changing big data to provide such updates. (Courtesy of Hopper, 2016, http://www.hopper.com/.)

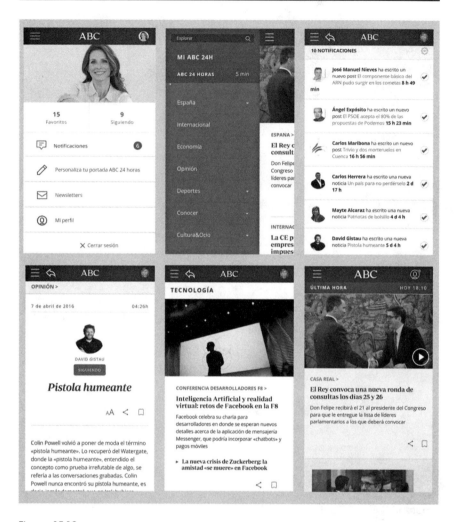

Figure 15.12

Diario ABC app, designed by Chaotic Moon Studios. With consistent branding through color and layout, this app triggers subtle changes to generate hierarchy. For example, the last screenshot on the bottom right is breaking news, so the page is colored off-white to signal this to the reader. In addition, user profiles provide customized access to the news. (Courtesy of FJORD, 2016, https://www.fjordnet. com/workdetail/abc-mobile/.)

Figure 15.13

Diario ABC app for the Apple Watch provides listening and saving functions for selected news, offering at least two headlines at once. (Courtesy of Vocento, S. A., 2016, Diario ABC on the App Store, *App Store*, https://itunes.apple.com/us/app/diario-abc/id336860348?mt=8.)

References

Bridge Design Inc. 2016. Touch Screen Ergonomics: The Key to Seamless Usability. Accessed January 10, 2016. http://bridgedesign.com/touch-screen-ergonomics/.

FJORD. 2016. A Made to Measure Newspaper for You ... and Your Smartphone. Accessed December 26, 2016. https://www.fjordnet.com/workdetail/abc-mobile/.

Frog. 2016. Smart Toys | Frog. Accessed December 23, 2016. http://www.frogdesign.com/work/yibu.html.

Hopper. 2016. When to Fly and Buy on Hopper. Accessed December 26, 2016. http://www.hopper.com/.

Huge. 2016. Website. Accessed December 23, 2016. http://www.hugeinc.com/case-study/up-next.

STREAKS. 2016a. The To-Do List That Helps You Form Good Habits. For iPhone. Accessed December 26, 2016. https://streaksapp.com/.

STREAKS. 2016b. The To-Do List That Helps You Form Good Habits. For iPhone. Accessed December 26, 2016. https://streaksapp.com/.

STREAKS. 2016c. The To-Do List That Helps You Form Good Habits. For iPhone. Accessed December 26, 2016. https://streaksapp.com/.

UCOP. 2016. Mobile Phones and Tablet Tips | UCOP. Accessed December 23, 2016. http://www.ucop.edu/risk-services/loss-prevention-control/ergonomics/ergo-mobile.html.

Vocento, S. A. 2016. Diario ABC on the App Store. *App Store*. Accessed December 26, 2016. https://itunes.apple.com/us/app/diario-abc/id336860348?mt=8.

16

Designing for Augmented Reality, Virtual Reality, and Mixed Reality

In 1968, Ivan Sutherland, with the help of his student Bob Sproull, invented and developed the first head-mounted display system for virtual and augmented reality, called the "Sword of Damocles." This device provided an early UI and graphics in an environment never before explored, a truly groundbreaking scientific achievement that the commercial world ignored at the time.

Later, in the mid-1970s, Myron Krueger took the lead in exploring artificial reality, creating in a laboratory called *Videoplace* an artificial reality with which users interacted through goggles and gloves. The environment provided projections and video cameras, and users could see their actions on the screen. In the early 1990s, the term *augmented reality* (AR) was first coined by researchers Tom Caudell and David Mizell. Developed off and on in various other projects, AR had a breakthrough in 2014 when Google started selling the mass-produced Google Glass device.

AR is now one of the fastest-growing fields, with investors in 2015 and 2016 giving companies working on AR over $700 million and $1.1 billion, respectively (Augment 2016). These numbers definitely indicate the future of interfaces. For further insight, see Chapter 18.

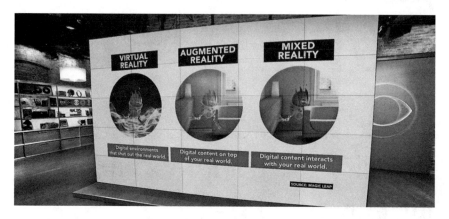

Figure 16.1

Differences between virtual reality, augmented reality, and mixed reality. (Courtesy of YouTube, 2016, https://www.youtube.com/user/CBSThisMorning.)

Comparison of AR, Virtual Reality, and Mixed Reality

Virtual reality (VR) is a 100% connected space, whether a 360° video, photo, or 3D environment. Completely separated from it physically, we are fully immersed in experiencing the environment because our minds are visually tricked. Meanwhile, AR adds images, videos, or any digital environment on top of our environment, which we can still see. Finally, mixed reality (MR) merges created digital content such as images or videos within our reality (Figure 16.1).

Human Factors for Spatial Interfaces

Convergence/Focus

When creating interfaces in AR, VR, or MR, find a balance of distance between the user and any digital object. Placing digital objects too close to the eyes will strain them and can harm vision over time. This is a very delicate rule to follow that must be considered throughout this type of interface design. In the real world, any object placed around 6 inches from our eyes becomes blurry and causes irritation, because we are trying to focus on something that is too close. Our eyes respond the same way when interacting with digital objects (Figure 16.2).

Distance

In the 3D environments of virtual realities, the interface display can be placed further away from or closer to the viewer. Set limitations so the user does not strain their eye muscles from viewing objects too close or too far away.

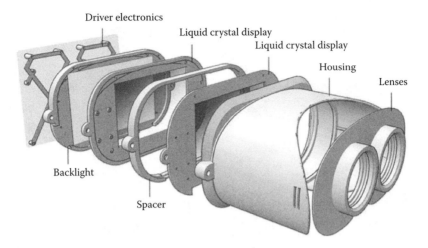

Driver electronics
Liquid crystal display
Liquid crystal display
Housing
Lenses
Backlight
Spacer

Figure 16.2

4D light lenses for virtual reality. (Courtesy of Ackerman, E., 2015, 4-D light field displays are exactly what virtual reality needs, *IEEE Spectrum: Technology, Engineering, and Science News*, http://spectrum.ieee.org/tech-talk/consumer-electronics/gaming/4d-light-field-displays-are-exactly-what-virtual-reality-needs.)

Scale

Interpupillary distance is a measurement of the distance between the pupils that sets the viewer's sense of scale. Decisions about scale will vary with the purpose of a UI, but make sure the scale of the environment has the proper proportion. If you are creating a game environment, like Alice in Wonderland, you can be more playful and explorative, but otherwise the user will be expecting a human scale.

Field of View and Position

The setting and perspective of the environment with which the user interacts can vary. In a first-person visual experience, the user directly experiences the interface. In a third-person visual experience, the user experiences the environment as another person, with their avatar actually in the environment.

Regarding field of view (FOV), there are two broad types, monocular and binocular (Figure 16.3). A binocular view has a broader view from 200 to 220 degrees, but we are only capable of capturing this broader perspective with our eyes when using both of them—monocular fields—in 3D. As a result, we have 114 degrees of view. Meanwhile, the monocular mode of a healthy eye, which is a horizontal FOV, is 170–175 degrees.

In addition, our nasal FOV varies with the size of our noses, ranging from 60 to 65 degrees of view. The FOV toward the sides of our head is 100–110 degrees ("Field of View for Virtual Reality Headsets Explained," 2016b).

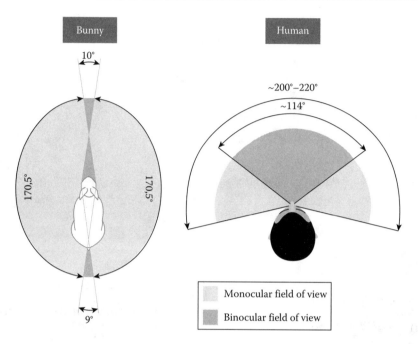

Figure 16.3

Monocular and binocular fields of view from rabbit and human perspectives. (Courtesy of VR Lens Lab, 2016a, https://vr-lens-lab.com/field-of-view-for-virtual-reality-headsets/.)

Motion Sickness

Avoid rapid or unstable movement that can make the user sick. If such motion is really required, warn users first. Identify actions that may cause motion sickness during prototype testing. People may become scared of heights, falling, large empty places, and darkness. Maintaining a stable horizon may help users avoid motion sickness.

Maintain Head Tracking

At all times, make sure the user remains aware of location. Have navigational features so the user can navigate through or exit different environments.

Shutting Down

When creating virtual reality interfaces, let users know when something is wrong, whether through an interstitial or a window that visually reports a glitch or some type of error.

Parallax Effect

The parallax effect can really help create a sense of depth when scrolling or moving from left to right or top to bottom. It must be done in time, as abrupt breaks from consistency become bumpy, an effect almost like an earthquake passing through our eyes. As designers, we must control these experiences to make them as smooth and close to reality itself as possible.

Accelerating and Decelerating Velocity

Whether menu or window movement or running in a game experience, alert the user in advance of these changes. The ideal is to give users control over the speed, so that they can experience the changes at a slower pace if desired.

Tolerance

Different users will tolerate these new reality environments differently. Some people may not be able to stay in these environments for more than 20 minutes. Regardless, the eye muscles need time to adapt to these new environments, so test new interfaces with various types of people. Their tolerance will greatly impact the usage of the new interface. If only 20% of users can tolerate your new interface, you must make the interface more adaptable and easier for the user.

Resolution

The resolution in a virtual environment is very flexible, because it changes according to the horizontal, vertical, and depth dimensions of the digital object with which the user is interacting. Various AR companies have set an official standard pixel density of 60×60 pixels per degree, which means a total of $12,600 \times 6,000$ pixels in a 210×100 degree FOV (Figure 16.4).

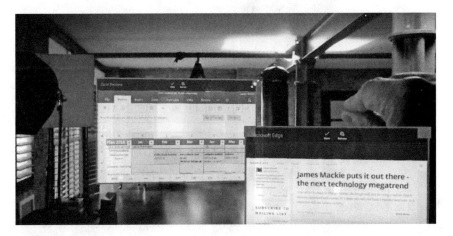

Figure 16.4

Resizing windows with AR using Microsoft HoloLens. In this demonstration, over several different windows are open from left to right, and the user has over 100 inches of width in screen resolution. Using VR makes accessible a flexible wider space than a screen, which is limited in size and space. (Courtesy of YouTube, 2016, https://www.youtube.com/watch?v=ihKUoZxNCIA.)

Virtual and Mixed Realities

WebVR

WebVR reaches one of the largest groups of users worldwide, because the Internet is already connecting us globally. Over 3 billion users could potentially have access to WebVR in the future. The Oculus VR lenses access an application called the *Carmel VR Browser*, which allows users access to the VR web. Others include the HTC Vive, Samsung Gear VR, and Google Cardboard. Many companies are expanding their websites to a VR mode, including WordPress, Amazon, Facebook, and Second Life (Figure 16.5).

Figure 16.5

Different types of Google Cardboard VR glasses. (Courtesy of Google VR, 2016, https://vr.google.com/cardboard/.)

Many YouTube videos are becoming available with Google Cardboard. By pressing the Google Cardboard icon (Figure 16.6), as long as the Google Cardboard app is downloaded on the user's phone and the phone is placed inside of the Google Cardboard device, the user can immerse themselves in the VR experience. Google has also embraced the Google Expeditions project, a VR app that allows field trips to many places worldwide. This app has been received very well among students and in various types of classroom learning environments.

What Are Holograms?

Holograms are 3D digital images created by light fields rather than formed by a lens. Laser light is required, because its wavelength does not change. Usually viewed in the dark, holograms are used in VR and MR (Figure 16.7).

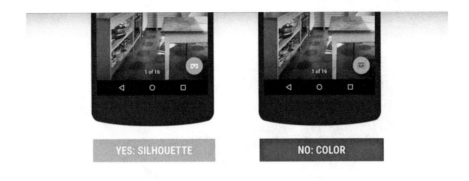

Figure 16.6

Google Cardboard icon shown in the interface. (Courtesy of YouTube, 2016, https://www.youtube.com/user/GoogleDevelopers.)

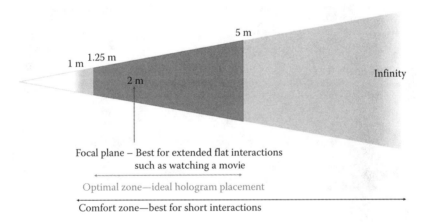

Figure 16.7

Diagram showing the best distance in green to place holograms from the user's perspective. (Courtesy of vo.msecnd.net, 2016, https://az835927.vo.msecnd.net/sites/holographic/resources/images/Comfortzone.JPG.)

In mixed reality, designers have more options as they can design icons or images in either 3D or 2D. To make the right decision between them, consider the concept in depth and analyze which way, 2D or 3D, the UI will be more effective. A decision to make an interface element 2D or 3D without thinking it through can be a disaster that requires a designer to start over. Again, testing from very early stages is important (Figures 16.8 and 16.9).

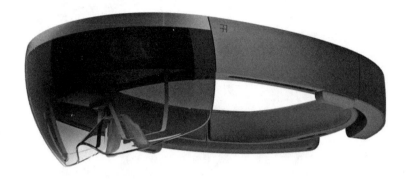

Figure 16.8

The Microsoft HoloLens provides MR experiences. (Courtesy of Microsoft, Redmond, WA, USA, 2016, https://www.microsoft.com/microsoft-hololens/en-us.)

Figure 16.9

Microsoft HoloLens experience. (Courtesy of YouTube, 2016, https://www.youtube.com/watch?v=L1ecfMWd9pg.)

Mixed Reality

MR means combining the physical world with digital holograms, in a way of interacting with both worlds at once.

Magic Leap is one of the largest, best-funded companies that is rapidly growing to create MR environments, including their own glasses version (Figure 16.10). The resolution and graphics in MR are of incredibly high quality.

Figure 16.10

Magic Leap.

UI Design

VR, AR, and MR interfaces are completely different from the old UI environments such as those for phones and desktops. Those used screens and had a limited canvas. These new environments use light and no screen, which creates flexibility in so many ways.

Contrast

Work with dimmer tones, as shown in Figure 16.11. Using bright white and a black background as contrast is not recommended (Figure 16.12), because this will strain the eye muscles.

Figure 16.11

Good contrast in color creates a visual hierarchy and balance in the interface (part of Oculus Guidelines by Kristoffer Brady and Richard Emms, Oculus).

Figure 16.12

Too-bright contrast in *Oculus Best Practices* by Kristoffer Brady, Lead Product Designer, Oculus, and Richard Emms, Designer & Creative Coder, Oculus.

Scrolling

Using vertical scroll, whether fast or slow, can cause motion sickness in VR (Figures 16.13 and 16.14). It is better instead to slide from left to right or left to bottom.

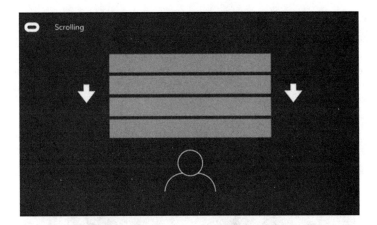

Figure 16.13

Scrolling in VR, AR, and MR is a negative visual experience in the Oculus Guidelines. (Courtesy of Kristoffer Brady and Richard Emms, Oculus.)

Figure 16.14

Moving UI: Swiping right to left (or left to right) is a positive visual experience in VR, AR, and MR (part of the Oculus Guidelines). (Courtesy of Kristoffer Brady and Richard Emms, Oculus.)

Navigation

Navigation should be placed in the most intuitive and accessible area, with suggested placement on the left or right side. In addition, do not design the space with windows placed everywhere, which can become overwhelming to the user.

Window Transitions

Transitions should be very smooth to avoid user confusion about the location of open or closed windows.

Differing z-Depths

With new options in 3D software, layers can provide distance by creating depth. Designers can use depth to create hierarchy among and balance the distance of digital objects, such as windows and icons. Place objects in the distance closer to each other, creating foreground and background, because human eyesight has limited sight at distance (Figure 16.15).

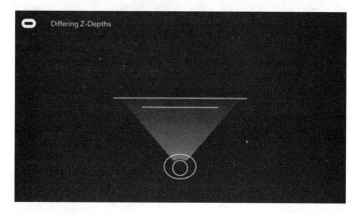

Figure 16.15

Differing z-depths provide a positive visual experience when windows or objects are close to each other in z-depth distance (part of the Oculus Guidelines by Kristoffer Brady and Richard Emms, Oculus).

Hovering/Click

Be aware that users' hands will most likely be interacting with an interface. Therefore, every time the user opens a window or selects something, maintain some type of visual hierarchy through color, size, transparency, or position.

Motion

Motion is a very challenging topic in virtual environments, because our physiology and eyes have expectations about the environment's response. Research continues to guide wayfinding and explore how our eyes can perceive closing, opening, adding, or deleting more intuitively without causing harm to any user. Therefore, testing is essential to create intuitive motion that will not cause harm or frustration for users. Options to speed up or slow down motion in spatial environments are very helpful, as users have various levels of behavior.

Audio

Interfaces involve audio in a limited way, to alert the user or let them know they are already in a different part of the interface. Audio is more used for media players, long motion, and interactivity, such as in a game or an immersive experience. Place sound in a strategic area of the environment. As shown in Figures 16.16 and 16.17, direct sound has various first-, second-, and third-order reflections.

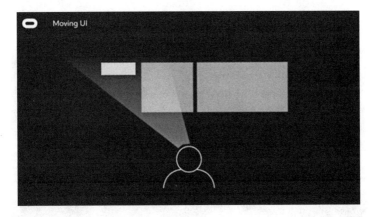

Figure 16.16

An appearing tab or menu can be created through motion when the tab appears and has a higher hierarchical order through color (part of the Oculus Guidelines by Kristoffer Brady and Richard Emms, Oculus).

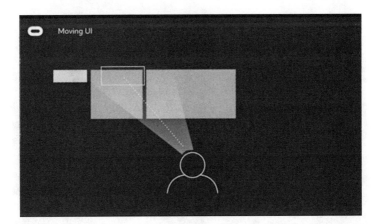

Figure 16.17

Motion in the UI is done by swiping left to right—a positive visual experience (in the Oculus Guidelines by Kristoffer Brady and Richard Emms, Oculus).

Wayfinding

Create a beginning and end. Let the user explore the space, and make sure there is an exit button at all times.

Prototyping Mazes in VR

When the interface has 2D graphics, it embraces a much larger group of people, including the elderly. A study (Figures 16.18–16.21) found that the over-60 population were not able to submerge themselves into the 3D maze VR experience. Younger people, on the other hand, were able to experience VR, especially the 20–40 age group.

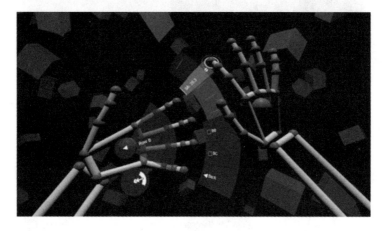

Figure 16.18

Cascading menu—a dynamic user VR interface is a Hover UI Kit tool.

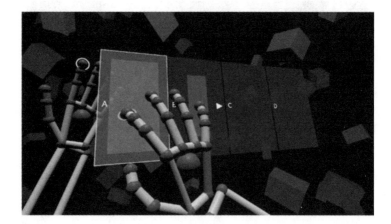

Figure 16.19

Window menu panels of a dynamic user VR interface is a Hover UI Kit tool.

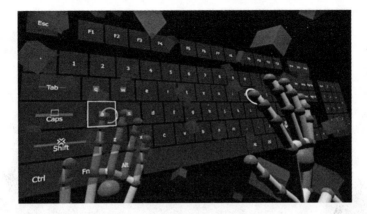

Figure 16.20

VR keyboard of a dynamic user VR interface is a Hover UI Kit tool.

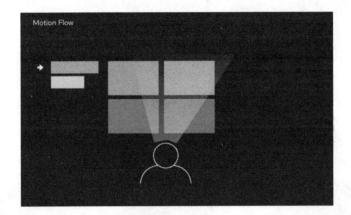

Figure 16.21

Motion flow: A link in the menu is highlighted, as is the location of the window desired by the user. (Courtesy of Oculus Guidelines by Kristoffer Brady and Richard Emms, Oculus; Courtesy of aestheticinteractive, 2016, https://github.com/aestheticinteractive/Hover-UI-Kit.)

Prototyping for VR

When prototyping for VR, use 3D software that allows you to set cameras and work in the x, y, and z dimensions, such as Unity, Vuforia, After Effects, Maya, and Cinema 4D, among others (Figures 16.22–16.28).

Icons

Icons are very necessary in VR interfaces, and the user needs to know where they are, whether in an accessible place close to their hands or very close to their eyesight.

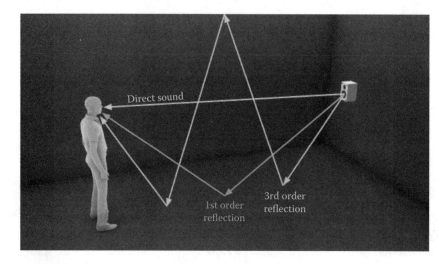

Figure 16.22

Spatial audio for Google VR. (Courtesy of aestheticinteractive, 2016, https://github.com/aestheticinteractive/Hover-UI-Kit; Courtesy of Google Developers, 2016, *Spatial Audio | Google VR | Google Developers*, https://developers.google.com/vr/concepts/spatial-audio.)

(a)   (b)

Figure 16.23

(a) Egocentric and (b) allocentric space in game design.

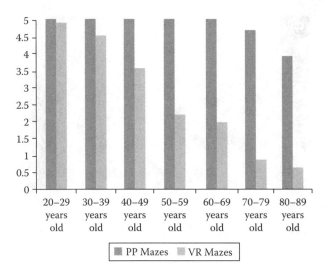

Figure 16.24

VR maze study for a wide range of ages, from 20 to 89 years old.

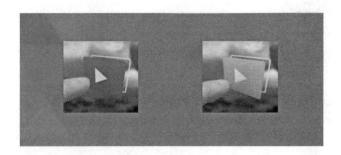

Figure 16.25

2D icons being tested in VR. (Courtesy of MikeAlger, 2016, http://mikealger.com/.)

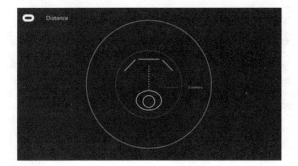

Figure 16.26

The visual experiences from 1 to 2 meters and 1 to 5 meters are the best for the user.

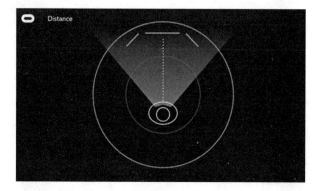

Figure 16.27

The interfaces located on the left and right side of the user's eye need to be placed in an angle for better legibility.

Figure 16.28

VR elevator technology by ThyssenKrupp Elevator AG. ThyssenKrupp uses HoloLens technology to help over 24,000 servicemen to do their jobs faster and more safely. The HoloLens provides a lot of information about each elevator. Andreas Schierenbeck, CEO of ThyssenKrupp, said: "Our goal is to increase efficiency, to increase the availability of our elevators and to optimize our service so that the technology of the lifts always works optimally." (Courtesy of Virtual Reality, 2016, http://www.virtual-reality-magazin.de/aufzuege-warten-mit-mixed-reality; courtesy of ThyssenKrupp Elevator, Essen, Germany, 2016, https://www.thyssenkrupp-elevator.com/en/.)

References

Ackerman, Evan. 2015. 4-D light field displays are exactly what virtual reality needs. *IEEE Spectrum: Technology, Engineering, and Science News.* Accessed August 14, 2016. http://spectrum.ieee.org/tech-talk/consumer-electronics/gaming/4d-light-field-displays-are-exactly-what-virtual-reality-needs.

aestheticinteractive. 2016. aestheticinteractive/Hover-UI-Kit. *GitHub.* Accessed December 27, 2016. https://github.com/aestheticinteractive/Hover-UI-Kit.

Anders, Peter. 2008. Designing mixed reality: Perception, projects and practice. *Technoetic Arts* 6(1): 19–29.

Augment. 2016. Infographic: The history of augmented reality—Augment news. *Augment News.* Accessed May 12, 2016. http://www.augment.com/blog/infographic-lengthy-history-augmented-reality/.

Campos, Pedro, and Sofia Pessanha. 2011. Designing augmented reality tangible interfaces for kindergarten children. *Lecture Notes in Computer Science* 6773, 12–19.

Chen, Ian Yen-hung, Bruce A. Macdonald, and Burkhard C. Wünsche. 2010. Designing a Mixed Reality Framework for Enriching Interactions in Robot Simulation. In: *Proceedings of the International Conference on Computer Graphics Theory and Applications.* doi: http: //dx.doi.org/10.5220/0002817903310338.

Google Developers. 2016. *Spatial Audio | Google VR | Google Developers.* Accessed December 27, 2016. https://developers.google.com/vr/concepts/spatial-audio.

Google VR. 2016. *Google Cardboard.* Accessed December 27, 2016. https://vr.google.com/cardboard/.

Huang, Weidong, Leila Alem, and Mark A. Livingston. 2012. *Human Factors in Augmented Reality Environments.* Springer Science & Business Media, Sebastopol, CA.

Jerald, Jason. 2015. *The VR Book: Human-Centered Design for Virtual Reality.* Morgan & Claypool Publishers-ACM, San Rafael, CA.

Laviola, Joseph J., Doug A. Bowman, Ernst Kruijff, Ryan P. McMahan, and Ivan Poupyrev. 2016. *3D User Interfaces: Theory and Practice.* Addison-Wesley Professional, Sebastopol, CA.

Microsoft. 2016. *Microsoft HoloLens.* Accessed December 26, 2016. https://www.microsoft.com/microsoft-hololens/en-us.

MikeAlger. 2016. Accessed December 27, 2016. http://mikealger.com/.

Parisi, Tony. 2015. *Learning Virtual Reality: Developing Immersive Experiences and Applications for Desktop, Web, and Mobile.* O'Reilly Media, Inc., Sebastopol, CA.

ThyssenKrupp. 2016. Your Global Urban Mobility Leader—ThyssenKrupp Elevator. Accessed December 27, 2016. https://www.thyssenkrupp-elevator.com/en/.

Virtual Reality. 2016. *Aufzüge Warten Mit Mixed Reality | Virtual Reality Magazin.* Accessed December 27, 2016. http://www.virtual-reality-magazin.de/aufzuege-warten-mit-mixed-reality.

vo.msecnd.net. 2016. Accessed December 26, 2016. https://az835927.vo.msecnd. net/sites/holographic/resources/images/Comfortzone.JPG.

VR Lens Lab. 2016. Field of View for Virtual Reality Headsets Explained. Accessed March 17, 2016. https://vr-lens-lab.com/field-of-view-for-virtual-reality-headsets/.

YouTube. 2016. CBS This Morning. 2016. Accessed December 26, 2016. https://www.youtube.com/user/CBSThisMorning.

YouTube. 2016. Google Developers. Accessed December 26, 2016. https://www.youtube.com/user/GoogleDevelopers.

YouTube. 2016. *Microsoft HoloLens Experience*. Accessed April 24, 2017. https://www.youtube.com/watch?v=L1ecfMWd9pg.

YouTube. 2016. *Microsoft HoloLens Review, Mind Blowing Augmented Reality!* Accessed April 24, 2017. https://www.youtube.com/watch?v=ihKUoZxNClA.

17

Design Development

The design development stage is one of the most rewarding experiences once you have completed the entire process from sketching to designing the visual experience. Your project workflow must be organized so that the developers can understand how the images, fonts, and layout will be arranged. Each client or company might request specifications following operating system guidelines (e.g., iOS, Android, or Daydream). Each different operating system has different regulations, as well as undergoing constant growth and change. Designer and developer must work together to make the transition from design prototype to developed prototype.

The designer must explain how the interactivity should work, as well as, making images ready for placement in the application. Use the guidelines of the operating system for which you are designing. For example, when designing an app for Android, follow Android guidelines in everything, including image sizes, icons, and resolution. The example in Figures 17.1 through 17.3 shows how to prepare your files for iOS, Android, and the web. If you are creating an application for a custom system, look at its guidelines and the rules behind it. There is UI prototyping software that can make your life easier, such as InVision in Figures 17.1 through 17.3.

During the delivery process, all files must have good resolution and the correct hierarchy. Typefaces and the design patterns must also be well organized (Figures 17.4–17.6).

Figure 17.1

Developer notes when they receive UI design. (Courtesy of InVision, 2016a, https://www.invisionapp.com/feature/inspect.)

Figure 17.2

InVision is a prototyping tool that provides a plugin called *Inspect* to help the designer prepare a better file for the developer that includes detailed measurements of distances for icons and text, even including Cascading Style Sheets (CSS). (Courtesy of InVision, 2016b, https://www.invisionapp.com/feature/inspect.)

Figure 17.3

Close-up version of the Inspect part of InVision. (Courtesy of InVision, 2016c, https://www.invisionapp.com/feature/inspect.)

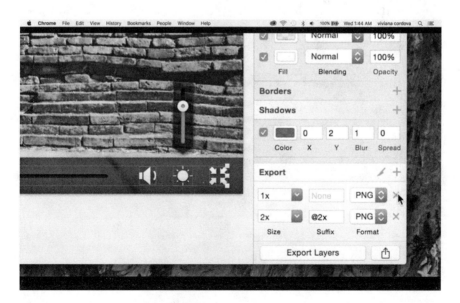

Figure 17.4

Sketch, a prototyping app, has options to export graphics for 1x and 2x. (Courtesy of Sketch, 2016, https://www.sketchapp.com/.)

Figure 17.5

Sketch, a prototyping app, has options to export files, including every detail and CSS. (Courtesy of Sketch, 2016, https://www.sketchapp.com/.)

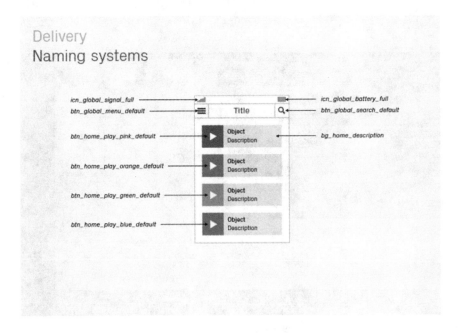

Figure 17.6

Pixel Perfect Precision delivery naming systems guideline sheet. (Courtesy of ustwo, 2016, https://ustwo.com/.)

It's All about the Resolution!

When preparing and exporting images, the most important part is to know the right size and quality of resolution. At the moment, the maximum quality resolution of pixel density is 3× and the minimum is 1× for tablet and smartphone resolutions. The most-used file extensions are PNG (raster image) and SVG (vector image) (Figures 17.7–17.9).

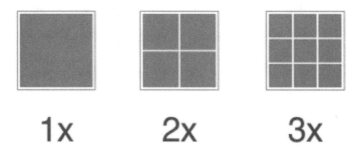

1x   2x   3x

Figure 17.7

Resolution of icons needed for the three types of screen resolution in all mobile interfaces.

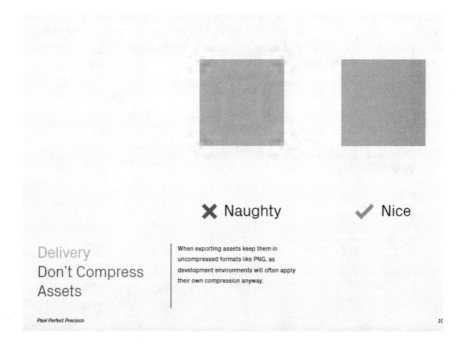

Figure 17.8

Carefully check that all images, animations, and videos have the resolution needed for the operating system. (Courtesy of ustwo, 2016, https://ustwo.com/.)

Submission Requirements

Please save each of the following assets in a PNG-24/32 file.

Asset Sizes: 1. Landscape (16:9) - *2560x1440px*
2. Square (1:1) - *1440x1440px*
3. Portrait (7:10) - *1008x1440px*
4. VR Landscape (3:1) - *1080x360px*

File Types: Production File - PNG-24/32

Please be sure to maintain the legibility of your logo across each asset size.

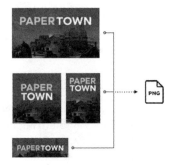

Figure 17.9

File preparation guidelines for Oculus VR. (Courtesy of Oculus Store Art Guidelines, 2016, https://static.oculus.com/documents/oculus-store-art-guidelines.pdf.)

Branding

The development team must be aware of the limitations and design guidelines of the identity system (Figure 17.10). Once the client agrees to the final identity system for the brand, follow the system carefully so the branding becomes consistent, successful, and reliable.

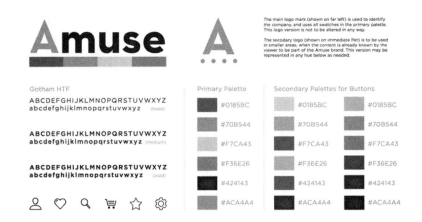

Figure 17.10

Part of the branding style guide for the Amuse app, designed by Erika Hagen and Collin McConnell.

17. Design Development

Communication

Learning to collaborate is an art in itself! The developer already has a lot of work to do in programming the design. As the designer, make his or her life simpler by having an organized set of folders and size details for the layout. Stay in touch with the developer from the beginning to the end of the project, because the developer will give you feedback on the time and expense required to make your UI design happen. Be prepared to be flexible and make a change if something happens at the last minute. Nothing is perfect in design. If we had infinite time, we could continue to make changes, but tight deadlines and awareness of the developer's limited time means you must communicate with each other and stay aware of deadlines. Submitting files does not end your part of the project. There is always something that might need to be revised. As long as the UI is published, the designer must be ready to make changes and revisions for it to be successful.

References

InVision. 2016a. Inspect—Pixel-Perfect Design Handoffs for Your Team. Accessed December 27, 2016. https://www.invisionapp.com/feature/inspect.

InVision. 2016b. Inspect—Pixel-Perfect Design Handoffs for Your Team. Accessed December 27, 2016. https://www.invisionapp.com/feature/inspect.

InVision. 2016c. Inspect—Pixel-Perfect Design Handoffs for Your Team. Accessed December 27, 2016. https://www.invisionapp.com/feature/inspect.

Oculus Store Art Guidelines. 2016. Accessed December 27, 2016. https://static.oculus.com/documents/oculus-store-art-guidelines.pdf.

ustwo. 2016. *Ustwo | Digital Product Studio.* Accessed December 27, 2016. https://ustwo.com/.

18

Conclusion

Interface design has dramatically changed entertainment, education, social relationships, and entire environments and human behavior. We have adjusted to new ways of receiving, sharing, interacting, creating, and sending information. The Information Age is here, expanding to the four corners of the earth and beyond. Moving into the Singularity Era, information will explode further. People innovating in the UI field have the responsibility to share and build upon what is being discovered. I believe that open source information has been the key to the successful growth of the visual experience field, which includes not only graphic designers but also animators, computer scientists, sociologists, and more. Technology will be making huge leaps over the next 10–20 years, with digital natives increasingly comfortable in their own virtual-reality environments.

Muriel Cooper, a renowned graphic designer and professor at Massachusetts Institute of Technology (MIT), started the Visible Language Workshop in the early 1980s. The workshop highlighted the future of typography, the information landscape, and how to interact with information in dimensional spaces. The information landscape was a new interface design for text that the user could virtually fly through. At that time, it was overwhelming to see an interface with no boundaries compared to contemporary 2D websites with their very restricted layouts. Her futuristic vision is now becoming reality (Figures 18.1 through 18.3).

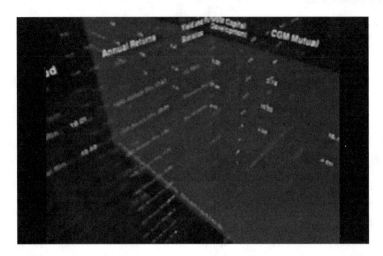

Figure 18.1

Still from Muriel Cooper's Visual Language Workshop.

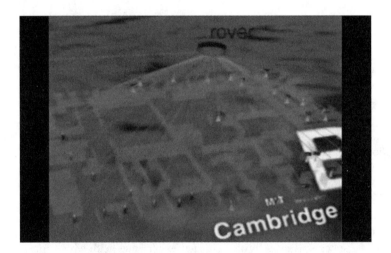

Figure 18.2

Still from Muriel Cooper's Visual Language Workshop.

The rapid, exponential growth in computing memory and speed each year has helped new and better-resolution interface environments to evolve almost everywhere in the world.

Interdisciplinary work is needed now more than ever. More complex systems require more knowledge about our users, whether obtained through psychology, ethnography, social sciences, behavioral sciences, linguistics, environmental science, or interior design. We will need to work on teams with various specialties to help resolve UI problems.

Figure 18.3

Still from Muriel Cooper's Visual Language Workshop at MIT. (Courtesy of YouTube, 2010, Information Landscapes, https://www.youtube.com/watch?v=Qn9zCrlJzLs.)

In addition, the vast majority of people born in 2000 and beyond are digital natives, who will have high expectations for technology in the years to come. There is pressure for innovation to move forward, and in a huge step, digital natives are starting to become the voice of research and innovation at various emerging and growing companies, such as Google (Figures 18.4 and 18.5), Microsoft, Amazon, Automatic, and Samsung. We are reshaping the future to make the visual experiences of our daily routines simpler.

Figure 18.4

Tilt brush for VR by Google.

Figure 18.5

Tilt Brush for VR by Google. (Courtesy of Tilt Brush, 2016, Tilt Brush by Google, https://www.tilt brush.com/.)

In addition, the evolution of artificial intelligence is not only pushing us to new virtual realities but is also changing physical reality, with advanced robotics that themselves require interfaces. There is a call to interface designers to set new guidelines for visual experiences related to our physiology, especially our senses, which interact with everything around us. Robotics and superhuman development will allow us to interact with graphical interfaces more naturally through intuition and perception. Interface designers no longer only need to understand the essential tools of graphic design. We must push ourselves toward innovation, research, and interdisciplinary work.

References

Tilt Brush. 2016. Tilt Brush by Google. Accessed December 28, 2016. https://www. tiltbrush.com/.

YouTube. 2010. Information Landscapes. Accessed December 23, 2016. https:// www.youtube.com/watch?v=Qn9zCrIJzLs.

Index